GETTYSBURG

THE TRUE ACCOUNT OF TWO YOUNG HEROES
IN THE GREATEST BATTLE OF THE CIVIL WAR

Iain Cameron Martin

Sky Pony Press
New York

Author's Note: This book was written drawing on a number of original and secondary sources. Because this book is intended for younger readers, citations have been limited to listing the works used in the bibliography. Almost no changes have been made to any original quotations, only a few minor edits were made on behalf of contemporary readers. Any errors within are entirely my own.

Sky Pony Press books may be purchased in bulk at special discounts for sales promotion, corporate gifts, fund-raising, or educational purposes. Special editions can also be created to specifications. For details, contact the Special Sales Department, Sky Pony Press, 307 West 36th Street, 11th Floor, New York, NY 10018 or info@skyhorsepublishing.com.

Sky Pony® is a registered trademark of Skyhorse Publishing, Inc.®, a Delaware corporation.

Visit our website at www.skyponypress.com.

10 9 8 7 6 5 4 3 2 1

Manufactured in China, March 2012
This product conforms to CPSIA 2008

Library of Congress Cataloging-in-Publication Data
Martin, Iain C.
 Gettysburg : the true account of two young heroes in the greatest battle of the Civil War / Iain Cameron Martin.
     pages cm
 Includes bibliographical references and index.
 ISBN 978-1-62087-532-2 (hardcover : alk. paper) 1. Gettysburg, Battle of, Gettysburg, Pa., 1863--Juvenile literature. 2. Alleman, Tillie Pierce--Juvenile literature. 3. Skelly, Daniel, 1844-1932--Juvenile literature. 4. Pennsylvania--History--Civil War, 1861-1865--Social aspects--Juvenile literature. 5. United States--History--Civil War, 1861-1865--Social aspects--Juvenile literature. I. Title.
 E475.53.M36 2013
 973.7'349--dc23
                                         2013001086

Editor: Julie Matysik
Designer: Sara Kitchen
Layout: Victoria Hughes Waters

This book is dedicated to my father, Blair Robertson Martin,
for teaching me a love of history—and to my own little rebels, Thomas and Sofia.

Author's Note: Words that may be new to readers are highlighted with **bold** text the first time they appear on this book. You can find definitions to those words in the glossary at the end.

Contents

Civil War Army Organization

Military units of the Civil War varied greatly in size and composition. Army formations were often fighting under strength due to casualties, sickness, or desertions. In general, however, the following list explains the basic terms and size of Civil War army organization.

Battery: 4–6 cannons commanded by a lieutenant

Troop: 80–100 cavalry commanded by a captain

Company: 100 men commanded by a captain

Regiment: 800–1,000+ men, 10 companies commanded by a colonel

Brigade: 3,000–4,000+ men, 4–6 regiments commanded by a brigadier general

Division: 10,000–12,000 men, 3+ brigades commanded by a brigadier or major general

Corps: 20,000–30,000 men, 2–4 divisions commanded by a major general or a lieutenant general (Confederate corps were larger than their Union counterparts.)

Army: 1+ corps, led by a commanding general. (Union armies were typically named after the rivers in the territory where they operated. Confederate armies were named from the state or regions where they were active.)

In 1863, the Union Army of the Potomac had seven infantry corps. The Confederate Army of Northern Virginia had three infantry corps. All units were officially numbered but were often also identified by their commander's name. By 1863, many units were operating by as much as 50 percent under-strength.

Civil War Army Ranks

private

corporal

sergeant

lieutenant

captain

major

lieutenant colonel

colonel

brigadier general

major general

lieutenant general

general

Introduction

THE CROSSROADS OF OUR BEING

I first became interested in the Civil War when I was fifteen, the year I began attending a small boarding school in southern Pennsylvania called Mercersburg Academy. I quickly learned that one of the girls' dormitories—a brick structure well over a century old—was haunted. The building had been used as a field hospital during the Confederate army's retreat from Gettysburg. The ghosts that wandered those halls were said to be the departed souls of Confederate soldiers. That's when it dawned on me that just over forty miles to the east lay the greatest battlefield in American history.

On a cloudy fall day that same year my father drove me to Gettysburg where I stood on Cemetery Ridge for the first time. Standing near a row of westward-facing cannons we looked out across Emmitsburg Road and toward the open fields stretching almost a mile to Seminary Ridge. Over a century earlier, on July 3, 1863, General Robert E. Lee had ordered 12,000 men to cross that field and to take the high ground where we stood. Forever known after as Pickett's Charge, those brave Southern soldiers crossed that open mile under a lethal hail of cannon and musket fire to try to break the Union line.

Looking out over that vast space, I began to realize the true meaning of courage. The entire American Civil War unfolded for me on this single field—two great armies, brothers and friends divided by a cause neither would yield, a

> " In great deeds, something abides. On great fields, something stays. Forms change and pass; bodies disappear; but spirits linger, to consecrate ground for the vision-place of souls. And reverent men and women from afar, and generations that know us not and that we know not of, heart-drawn to see where and by whom great things were suffered and done for them, shall come to this deathless field, to ponder and dream . . . "
>
> —Joshua Lawrence Chamberlain

gallant rush for victory. I was desperate to know more. Here was a history worth learning. Considered **sacred** ground, and **consecrated** by the blood of Americans, the battlefield has become a national monument to unity and peace. It is a timeless place that can help connect us, over a century later, to important deeds of the past.

But why should we care about history that is 150 years in our past? America has moved onward. We are a modern nation of the digital age, with smartphones and hybrid cars. Why do we need to learn about these dusty old stories from our past? Is it really all that important to retell them to new generations? What do we benefit from doing so? And why do we care about a single battle from a nineteenth-century war? These are all valid questions.

Bruce Catton was a great Civil War historian who won the Pulitzer Prize for history in 1954. As a young boy growing up in the small town of Benzonia, Michigan, he would sit on the front porch of his neighbor's house and listen to the stories of Union veterans. Speaking in 1961 on the meaning of the Civil War, Catton noted, "It was the biggest single event in our national history. In a way it is the central theme of our existence as a people; it is our *Iliad*, our *Odyssey*, the one tremendous legend that expresses what we are and what we mean. We can no more ignore it than we can ignore the American Revolution itself. Here was our most significant and tragic experience."

If we are to understand ourselves as Americans and as a **unified** nation, we must have an understanding of the Civil War. Shelby Foote, an eminent historian from Mississippi, put it this way: "The Civil War defined us as what we are and it opened us to being what we became, good and bad things . . . It was the crossroads of our being, and it was a hell of a crossroads."

Gettysburg was one of the great turning points of American history. Certainly there were other battles and other turning points of equal importance that decided Union victory. Yet Gettysburg is the *one* battle Americans seem to remember the most. For the South, it was a supreme moment of honor, courage, and sacrifice for their cause of independence. For the North, it was another step toward what Lincoln called "a new birth of freedom." What **ultimately** emerged from the Civil War was a united country free of slavery. Today, looking back, we understand that the war between North and South is *the* American story and in every way worth knowing so that we might better understand ourselves and our country.

Gettysburg

The Emmitsburg road had been the last long mile for many men—for handsome John Reynolds riding to meet an unknown Southern sharpshooter in a farmer's barn, for the black-hatted Western regiments with their fife-and-drum corps playing them into battle, for many unheard-of men who stepped off it into unmarked graves on slanting rocky fields—and for a few days it had been a famous military highway, pumping a stream of troops off to the unfathomable chances of war. Now it would be a quiet country road again, with a farmer's load of hay or drove of cattle as its most exciting wayfarers, the mountain wall to the west dropping long shadows across it on the blue summer evenings, the dust and the clamor and the rumbling guns gone forever. It was over at last, this enormous battle with its smoke and its grimness and its unheard-of violence, and here again was a simple road leading from one country town to another, with a common-place little name that would ring and shine in the books forever.

—Bruce Catton

Prologue

"The Rebels are coming!
The Rebels are coming!"

Matilda "Tillie" Pierce looked up from her schoolwork as the shout went from room to room. Rushing to the door, she and the other girls gathered on the front **portico** of their school. In plain view, marching toward Gettysburg on the Chambersburg Pike, was a dusty mass of Confederate infantry. The teacher, Mrs. Eyster, turned to her students and ordered, "Children, run home as quickly as you can!"

Tillie ran for her father's house on Baltimore Street as Confederate riders entered the town. As she reached the front door, men on horseback appeared on her street.

Tillie Pierce in 1863 at age fifteen.
Photo credit: Adams County Historical Society.

Tillie Pierce's home on Baltimore Street as it stands today, restored to its 1863 appearance. Photo credit: Ken Giorlando.

I scrambled in, slammed shut the door, and hastening to the sitting room, peeped out between the shutters.

What a horrible sight! There they were, human beings! Clad almost in rags, covered with dust, riding wildly, pell-mell down the hill toward our home! Shouting, yelling most unearthly, cursing, brandishing their revolvers, and firing right and left.

I was fully persuaded that the Rebels had actually come at last.

Soon the town was filled with infantry, and then the searching and ransacking began in earnest.

They wanted horses, clothing, anything and almost everything they could conveniently carry away.

Nor were they particular about asking. Whatever suited them they took. They did, however, make a formal demand of the town authorities, for a large supply of flour, meat, groceries, shoes, hats, and ten barrels of whiskey; or, in lieu of all this, five thousand dollars.

But our merchants and bankers had too often heard of their coming, and had already shipped their wealth to places of safety.

—Tillie Pierce

The soldiers rounded up all the horses in town, including the one owned by Tillie's father. Then they returned to the house and asked for something to eat. Mrs. Pierce **scolded** them, saying, "Yes, you ought to come back and ask for something to eat after taking a person's horse!" She nevertheless gave them some food. As Tillie recalled, "Mother always had a kind and noble heart even toward her enemies."

Michael Jacobs, a professor at Pennsylvania College, witnessed the arrival of Confederate soldiers. Of the 5,000 troops of Brigadier General John B. Gordon's brigade, most of them "were exceedingly dirty, some ragged, some without shoes, and some surmounted by the skeleton of what was once an entire hat, affording unmistakable evidence that they stood in great need of having their scanty wardrobe replenished; and hence the eagerness with which they inquired after shoe, hat, and clothing stores, and their disappointment when they were informed that goods of that description were not to be had in town." In exchange for supplies that could be found, the troops often paid with Confederate money—printed bills not worth the paper they were cut from, unless of course, the South won the war.

By evening the raiders had moved all the freight cars near Gettysburg out to the railroad bridge east of town, then set it all on fire. In the morning the infantry was gone, marching twenty-five miles northeast toward York where General Ewell hoped to capture a bridge over the Susquehanna River. The townspeople wondered if they would return. Were other Confederates likely to pass through Gettysburg? And where was the Union army?

Baltimore Street in Gettysburg.
Photo credit: Ken Giorlando.

Chapter One
Lee's Plan— Attack into Pennsylvania

War consists not only in battles, but in well-considered movements which bring the same results.

—John C. Fremont

The soldiers who occupied Gettysburg that day were from Lieutenant General Richard S. Ewell's Second Corps of the Army of Northern Virginia. Advancing with two other corps from Fredericksburg, Virginia, through Maryland and into Pennsylvania, the Confederate army under General Robert E. Lee was on the offensive. Confident from victory over the Union's Army of the Potomac at Chancellorsville in May, Lee had championed the idea of a new invasion of the North. It was a bold plan to win Southern independence in a single campaign, and Confederate President Jefferson Davis was behind the **initiative**. Robert E. Lee was the Confederacy's greatest military commander. Graduating second in his class at West Point in 1829, Lee went on to serve in the corps of engineers. A **protégé** of General Winfield Scott, Lee served with valor and distinction under Scott during the Mexican War from 1846 to 1848. By the start of the Civil War, in April 1861, Lee was still only a colonel but already his reputation accorded him great respect.

General Robert E. Lee photographed in 1862 by Julian Vannerson. Photo credit: Library of Congress; illustrated by Ron Cole.

Robert Edward Lee was born on January 19, 1807, to Revolutionary War hero and Virginia Governor Henry "Light Horse" Harry Lee III and Anne Hill Carter at Stratford Hall Plantation, Virginia. One of six children, Lee began life in difficult times, losing his father when he was only eleven years old. With the help of relatives, Anne Carter raised the children herself and saw to their education.

A promising student of mathematics at an early age, Robert secured an appointment to the United States Military Academy at West Point when he was seventeen. There he distinguished himself by graduating second in his class in 1829. Two years later he married Mary Anna Randolph Custis, great-granddaughter of Martha Washington. They would have seven children over the years, three boys and four girls. All three of Lee's sons became officers in the Confederate army. Lee's wife inherited her father's estate in 1857, including the Arlington plantation across the Potomac from Washington, DC.

Lee served as a lieutenant of engineers at a number of civil projects until the Mexican War in 1846. That year he served as an aide to General Winfield Scott on his triumphant march from Vera Cruz to capture Mexico City. It was in this campaign that Lee earned **commendation** from the commanding general for his skill and courage as a scout. He also met and served with Ulysses S. Grant, to whom he would eventually surrender at Appomattox in 1865.

After the war Lee was promoted to colonel and served as the superintendent of West Point for three years. He finally received a combat command when he was assigned to the Second Cavalry regiment in Texas in 1855, where he faced off against Apache and Comanche raiders. He later commanded the **detachment** that put down John Brown's uprising at Harper's Ferry in 1859.

Robert E. Lee, around age forty-three, when he was a Brevet Lieutenant-Colonel of Engineers, c.1850. Photo credit: Matthew Brady.

After Texas seceded from the Union in February 1861, Lee returned to Washington and was appointed Colonel of the First Regiment of Cavalry in March.

Of utmost importance to Lee was adherence to duty. The idea that the South would attempt to leave the Union and form a new country troubled him deeply. He wrote to his son William Fitzhugh in 1861, "I can anticipate no greater **calamity** for the country than a dissolution of the Union." When asked by a friend if he intended to resign from the army to join the Confederacy he replied, "I shall never bear arms against the Union, but it may be necessary for me to carry a musket in the defense of my native state, Virginia."

The same day the Virginia state government met to debate joining the Confederacy on April 18, 1861, Lincoln offered Lee the rank of major general and command of the Union army. Yet, Lee knew that Lincoln was raising an army of volunteers to invade the South, and that Virginia would join the Confederacy. He refused to accept command of an army that would be ordered to invade his home.

Lee resigned from the United States Army on April 20, and accepted command of the Virginia state forces three days later. He wrote to his sister, "With all my devotion to the Union, and the feeling of loyalty and duty of an American citizen, I have not been able to make up my mind to raise my hand against my relative, my children, my home. I have, therefore, resigned my commission in the Army, and save in defense of my native State (with the sincere hope that my poor services may never be needed) I hope I may never be called upon to draw my sword."

Upon the formation of the Confederate States Army, Lee was promoted to one of its five full generals. A year later, Lee was given command of the Army of Northern Virginia on June 1, 1862, during the fighting against George McClellan's invasion of the peninsula. In the months that followed, Lee would prove more than a match for a succession of Union generals ordered south to try to capture Richmond.

An aide to Jefferson Davis once said that "Lee is **audacity** personified." The Gettysburg campaign was in every way an extension of Lee's character as a man of action. By the summer of 1863, the Army of Northern Virginia was at its strongest. Lee must have known that the tide of war would soon crush the Confederacy. He believed the attack into

Robert E. Lee, around age thirty-eight, and his son, William Henry Fitzhugh Lee, around age eight. Photo credit: Encyclopedia Virginia.

Pennsylvania was their best hope for winning independence while the South retained the initiative to make such a campaign.

Lee had every faith in his men and officers. He wrote of his soldiers before Gettysburg, "There never were such men—in any army before and there never can be better in any army again. If properly led, they will go anywhere and never falter at the work before them." Lee's belief in his men was central to his thinking when he ordered Pickett's Charge on July 3, at Gettysburg. His iron will could not accept the possibility of defeat on such a crucial field of battle.

When Lee surrendered to General Grant at Virginia's Appomattox Courthouse on April 9, 1865, they both set a tone for the reconciliation between the states that followed. Lee had refused the desire of many Confederate officers to disband the army and fight a guerrilla war against the federal government. Grant, in turn, gave Lee the most generous terms of surrender possible, allowing his troops to return to their homes. Lee also welcomed the end of slavery saying, "So far from engaging in a war to **perpetuate** slavery, I am rejoiced that slavery is abolished. I believe it will be greatly for the interests of the South."

Lee was revered by his soldiers more than any other American officer in history. An eyewitness to the surrender at Appomattox recorded, "When, after his interview with Grant, General Lee again appeared, a shout of welcome instinctively ran through the army. But, instantly recollecting the sad occasion that brought him before them, their shouts sank into silence, every hat was raised, and the bronzed faces of the thousands of grim warriors were bathed with tears. As he rode slowly along the lines, hun-

dreds of his devoted veterans pressed around the noble chief, trying to take his hand, touch his person, or even lay a hand upon his horse, thus exhibiting for him their great affection."

After the war, Lee would go on to great achievements in peace, accepting an offer to serve as the president of Washington College in Lexington, Virginia. Whatever his private misgivings were about the federal government he publicly supported reconciliation with the North and signed an oath of **allegiance** to the United States. Lee also appealed to President Johnson for an **amnesty** and pardon for his role in taking up arms against the government. His pardon was not granted until 1975 by President Gerald Ford.

Lee passed away on October 12, 1870, at the age of sixty-three in Lexington, Virginia. Over the years, Lee's memory became honored by both sides as a great general, a man of principle, and a man who, in the end, proved he was as equally great in the service of peace as in war. In 1874, Benjamin Harvey Hill described Lee as " . . . a foe without hate; a friend without treachery; a soldier without cruelty; a victor without oppression, and a victim without murmuring. He was a public officer without vices; a private citizen without wrong; a neighbor without reproach; a Christian without **hypocrisy**, and a man without **guile**. He was a Caesar, without his ambition; Frederick, without his tyranny; Napoleon, without his selfishness, and Washington, without his reward."

At the request of General Scott, Lincoln approved offering Lee command of the Union Army at the start of the war, but Lee knew that the army Lincoln was forming would be ordered into the southern states to put down the current rebellion. It would require that he turn against the people of his native state of Virginia. Lee decided this was something he could not do, so he resigned his commission in the United States Army and returned home.

Writing to his sister on April 20, 1861, Lee explained: "With all my devotion to the Union, and the feeling of loyalty and duty of an American citizen, I have not been able to make up my mind to raise my hand against my relative, my children, my home. I have, therefore, resigned my commission in the Army, and save in defense of my native State (with the sincere hope that my poor services may never be needed) I hope I may never be called upon to draw my sword." Three days after writing this letter, Lee accepted command of the military forces of Virginia. Within months he was promoted to one of only five full generals in the newly formed Confederate States Army.

Lee's first opportunity to lead an army in the field came a year later, in June 1862. Union

General Lee is, almost without exception, the handsomest man of his age I ever saw. He is fifty-six years old, tall, broad shouldered, very well made, well set up—a thorough soldier in appearance; and his manners are most courteous and full of dignity. He is a perfect gentleman in every respect. I imagine no man has so few enemies, or is so universally esteemed. Throughout the South, all agree in pronouncing him to be as near perfection as a man can be. He has none of the small vices, such as smoking, drinking, chewing, or swearing, and his bitterest enemy never accused him of any of the greater ones. He generally wears a well worn long gray jacket, a high black felt hat, and blue trousers tucked into his Wellington boots. I never saw him carry arms.

—Colonel Arthur James Lyon Fremantle

General George McClellan had landed the massive Federal army on the Virginia peninsula and was advancing toward Richmond. Confederate General Joseph E. Johnston, commanding the Army of Northern Virginia, was wounded in the early fighting and Lee was given command. Seizing the initiative, Lee attacked in what became known as the Battle of Seven Days, forcing McClellan's army back to the coast, where they eventually retreated to Maryland.

President Lincoln meets with General McClellan after the Battle of Antietam, October 3, 1862. Photo credit: Alexander Gardner, Library of Congress.

Major General George B. McClellan. Photo credit: Matthew Brady.

McClellan's defeat was a **humiliating** setback for Lincoln's war effort and a significant victory for Lee. The troops under his command realized they had a brilliant and daring general leading them, and they began calling him "Marse Lee"—a reference of respect as master. Over the next twelve months, three **decisive** Confederate victories were achieved under Lee's command: Second Manassas, Fredericksburg, and Chancellorsville.

In September 1862, Lee took his army into Maryland on his first invasion of the North. McClellan's Army of the Potomac attacked them at Antietam in what became the bloodiest day in American history. Lee's army fought with their backs to the Potomac River, crushing the Union assaults against their lines. Both sides suffered terrible losses, and Lee pulled his army back across the river into

Virginia to safety. Lee's daring and tactical skill saved his army from defeat, but their retreat to Virginia allowed Lincoln to claim this as a major Union victory.

Major General Ulysses S. Grant.
Photo credit: Matthew Brady.

Even with Lee's impressive victories, the war approached disaster for the Confederacy by 1863. The Union had seized control of the Upper Mississippi in February 1862, took key forts in Tennessee, and won a defensive battle at Shiloh. And much further to the south, Union forces had captured New Orleans in May 1862, cutting off the Mississippi to foreign trade and depriving the Confederacy of her most vital port.

By the summer of 1863, Grant was leading a **siege** against the fortress city of Vicksburg in Mississippi, defended by 30,000 Confederate soldiers. If Grant were to take this major river city, the entire Mississippi river would fall under Union control, splitting the Confederacy in two.

The strength of the Union army and northern industry was growing stronger while the Confederacy weakened. Every battle, victorious or not, cost the South thousands of men that could not be replaced. Time, it seemed, was running out for the South. Their only route to victory lay on the battlefield—so all eyes looked now to General Lee to deliver that victory, the one general who repeatedly crushed the Union armies sent to invade Virginia.

> *. . . Nothing gave me much concern so long as I knew that General Lee was in command. I am sure there can never have been an army with more supreme confidence in its commander than that army had in General Lee. We looked forward to victory under him as confidently as to successive sunrises.*
>
> —Colonel Edward Porter Alexander

Jefferson Davis, President of the Confederate States of America. Photo credit: National Archives.

Lee's plan was to move the Army of Northern Virginia north through the Blue Mountains using Major General J. E. B. Stuart's cavalry to screen their movements from the enemy. Once he crossed the Potomac River into Maryland, Lee would take his army into Pennsylvania, where they could "live off the enemy's land" and capture much-needed supplies. By threatening to occupy Harrisburg, the capital of Pennsylvania, Lee hoped to draw the Army of the Potomac out of Virginia and into the open fields where it could be decisively attacked. A major victory over the Army of the Potomac would likely draw Union forces away from the southern states, win foreign recognition, and even force Lincoln to the peace table.

Lee had every confidence in his men and in his own ability to defeat the enemy. Writing after his victory at Chancellorsville, Lee noted, "There never were such men—in any army before and there never can be better in any army again. If properly led, they will go

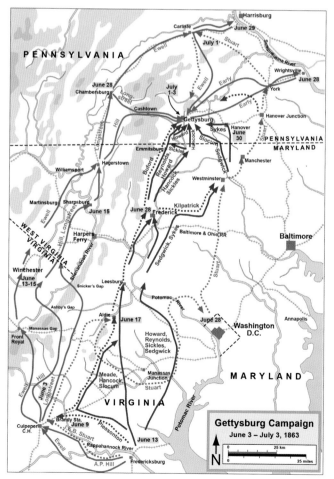

Map by Hal Jespersen, www.cwmaps.com.

anywhere and never falter at the work before them." An aide to President Jefferson Davis commented that "Lee is audacity personified." Lee now staked that reputation in an all-out campaign to bring the war to an end by invading the North.

OPENING MOVES—THE BATTLE FOR BRANDY STATION

On June 3, 1863, Lee's army slipped away from their defenses at Fredericksburg and

Major General James Ewell Brown "Jeb" Stuart. Photo credit: George S. Cook, National Archives.

Major General Joseph Hooker. Photo credit: Matthew Brady, Library of Congress.

moved northwest toward Culpeper, intending to cross the Rappahannock River and enter the Shenandoah Valley. Two days later, Major General Joseph Hooker, commanding the Army of the Potomac, received intelligence that Lee's forces were on the move. He telegraphed a message to his superiors in Washington, proposing an attack on Lee's defenses at Fredericksburg and then to move on to Richmond. President Lincoln immediately replied, "If Lee would come to my side of the river, I would keep on the same side, and fight him or act on the defense . . . Lee's army, and not Richmond, is your sure objective point."

During those first weeks of June, Lee's army was protected from Union view behind a screen of cavalry commanded by Major General J. E. B. Stuart. In an effort to break through and gain information on Lee's intentions, on June 9, General Hooker sent his own cavalry to make a surprise attack on Stuart's camps across the Rappahannock River at Brandy Station. In what became one of the largest cavalry battles in U.S. history, Hooker's effort almost succeeded. Stuart and his command were caught off guard by the dawn attack, but skillfully **rallied** a defense. By dusk,

the Union cavalry was compelled to withdraw north of the river, thus giving the Confederates a **tactical victory**.

Stuart claimed a victory, but the Richmond newspapers criticized his leadership. The *Richmond Enquirer* wrote that "General Stuart has suffered no little in public estimation by the late enterprises of the enemy." The *Richmond Examiner* described Stuart's command as "puffed up cavalry," that suffered the "consequences of negligence and bad management." Stuart was considered by many as the Confederacy's most brilliant cavalry leader and a national hero, so such harsh words cut him deeply. And this wounding of his pride would have **dire** consequences for the Pennsylvania campaign in the coming weeks.

The following day, Lee's Second Corps, under the command of Lieutenant General Richard S. Ewell, attacked the Federal garrison at Winchester, Virginia, capturing 4,000 prisoners, scores of supply wagons, horses, hundreds of rifles, and twenty-eight cannons. With the Confederate army now well supplied, the road north lay wide open for Lee's invasion. Ewell ordered his cavalry brigade into Pennsylvania as far north as Chambersburg. He wanted the faster moving mounted troops ahead of his corps to help raid and capture supplies.

Among the fallen from the battle at Winchester was Union Corporal Johnston "Jack" Skelly, a Gettysburg native. Mortally wounded, he wrote a farewell note to his fiancée back home—Mary Virginia Wade. By a stroke of good luck he met a close friend just before he died, Private Wesley Culp, another Gettysburg resident who vol-

Lieutenant General Richard Stoddert Ewell. Photo credit: National Archives.

Ewell is rather a remarkable looking old soldier, with a bald head, a prominent nose, and rather a haggard, sickly face; having so lately lost his leg above the knee, he is still a complete cripple, and falls off his horse occasionally.
—Colonel Arthur James Lyon Fremantle

Corporal Johnston "Jack" Skelly

The loss at Winchester stunned the North, and Pennsylvania Governor Andrew Curtin raised the call for 50,000 volunteers to defend the state against the Southern army's move north. Tillie Pierce wrote about Gettysburg's home grown **militia**: "I remember one evening in particular, when quite a number of them had assembled to guard the town that night against an attack from the enemy. They were 'armed to the teeth' with old, rusty guns and swords, pitchforks, shovels and pick-axes. Their falling into line, the maneuvers, the commands given and not heeded, would have done a **veteran's** heart good."

Private Wesley Culp

unteered for the Confederacy. Wesley had gone to school with both Jack and Mary. When he came across Jack at a field hospital the wounded soldier gave him a note to pass on to Mary.

Mary Virginia "Ginnie" Wade

Lieutenant Colonel Rufus Dawes

The Union veterans Tillie envisioned were at the moment setting out for Maryland and then Pennsylvania to confront Lee's army. Colonel Rufus Dawes was commander of the 6th Wisconsin, one of five **regiments** of the **elite** "Iron Brigade." In a letter to his fiancée on June 15, he wrote: "We are to march this morning positively. I think the whole army is going, for the order is from General Hooker . . . The regiment will go out strong in health and cheerful in spirit, and determined always to sustain its glorious history. It has been my ardent ambition to lead it through one campaign, and now the indications are that my opportunity has come."

EWELL'S SECOND CORPS CROSSES THE POTOMAC

On June 15, Ewell led his Second Corps across the Potomac River near Hagerstown, Maryland. His was the first Confederate corps to enter Pennsylvania a week later on the 22nd. Over the next week they marched through Greencastle to Chambersburg, then east to Gettysburg, where Tillie Pierce saw them for the first time, and northward to York County. Ewell's corps wanted to be in position for Lee to threaten Harrisburg, the state capital. Along the way, Ewell's troops **levied** towns for supplies of all kinds—food for the troops and horses for the cavalry. They took lots of property, even though Lee had ordered that nothing was to be seized or destroyed by his men outside the direct needs of the army. The order was quietly ignored by the hungry soldiers, but for an invading army, they took no revenge against the northern civilians—no homes were burned or families harmed.

Many of those who lost property in the wake of Lee's invasion fared better than civilians in the South, who had suffered during Federal occupation. At Fredericksburg in December 1862, undisciplined Union troops had pillaged the town. As the Army of the Potomac left Virginia to pursue Lee that summer of 1863, they left behind a countryside devastated by war.

The southerners were impressed by the Pennsylvania country through which they were

> *The country through which we passed towards Gettysburg seemed to abound chiefly in Dutch women who could not speak English, sweet cherries, and apple-butter. As we marched along, the women and children would stand at the front gate with large loaves of bread and a crock of apple-butter, and effectually prevent an entrance of the premises by the gray invaders. As I said before, the women could not talk much with us, but they knew how to provide "cut and smear," as the boys called it, in abundance.*
>
> —James Hodam, 17th Virginia Cavalry

marching. Summer was in full bloom with fields of waving wheat, orchards **laden** with ripe fruits, and quiet pastures of cattle beside the huge red barns of the Pennsylvania Dutch. Cavalryman James H. Hodam recalled, "The cherry crop was immense through this part of the state, and the great trees often overhung the highway laden with ripened fruit. The infantry would break off great branches and devour the cherries as they marched along."

On Sunday the 28th retreating Union militia set fire to the mile-long Columbia Bridge over the Susquehanna River to prevent its capture. "The scene was magnificent," wrote a reporter. "The moon was bright, and the blue clouds afforded the best contrast possible to the red glare of the **conflagration**. The light in the heavens must have been seen for many miles." By the next morning Ewell had received new orders from Lee. He would lead his men back the way they had come, south toward Gettysburg, and link up with A. P. Hill's and Longstreet's forces advancing eastward from Chambersburg.

LINCOLN'S COMMAND CRISIS

At the end of June, President Lincoln was concerned that Commanding General Hooker would lose his nerve when facing Lee a second time on the battlefield. Promoted to command after General Burnside's disaster at Fredericksburg in December 1862, Hooker had been quoted during the retreat by the *New York Times* as saying that "nothing would go right until we had a **dictator** and the sooner the better." A few weeks later Lincoln promoted Hooker to command the army and wrote to him, "I have heard, in such way as to believe it, of your recently saying that both the Army and the Government needed a Dictator. Of course it was not for this, but in spite of it, that I have given you the

President Abraham Lincoln painted by George Peter Alexander Healy. Photo credit: White House Collection.

confessed in a letter to his son Custis, "It is a terrible loss. I know not how to replace him."

General Hooker skillfully regrouped his army and had set them in motion to follow Lee's advance into Maryland, with five of his seven infantry corps ready to enter Pennsylvania and challenge Lee. But Lincoln could not afford to lose another battle. With his own officers questioning Hooker's ability to lead, the General knew he had also lost the confidence of the President and, thus, resigned command on June 28. Lincoln now chose Major General George Gordon Meade to replace Hooker. Only days before the largest battle of the Civil War, the Army of the Potomac suddenly had a new commander.

command. Only those generals who gain success can set up dictators. What I now ask of you is military success, and I will risk the dictatorship."

Three short months later, during the first week of May, Hooker failed to deliver that success and the Army of the Potomac had to retreat after General Lee's crushing victory at Chancellorsville. It was perhaps Lee's greatest victory, but also the costliest. Among the thousands of fallen soldiers was Lieutenant General Thomas "Stonewall" Jackson, Lee's greatest corps commander. After his death on May 10, Lee

Lieutenant General Thomas Jonathan "Stonewall" Jackson

Major General George Gordon Meade photographed by Matthew Brady. Photo credit: Library of Congress; illustrated by Ron Cole.

George Meade was born in Cadiz, Spain, the eighth child of eleven born to Richard Worsam Meade and Margaret Coats Butler. His father was from Philadelphia, and was a wealthy merchant serving in Spain as a naval agent for the United States. Financially ruined by the Napoleonic Wars, his father died when young George was not yet a teenager. The family, in danger of financial collapse, returned to the United States in 1828.

In part because West Point offered young men a free education, George entered the academy in 1831, graduating nineteenth in his class of fifty-six cadets in 1835. He served one year with the 3rd U.S. Artillery in Florida, fighting in the Seminole War before resigning his commission to begin a career as a civil engineer.

In 1840, George married Margaretta Sergeant who gave him seven children over the years. George returned to the army as a second lieutenant in the Corps of **Topographical** Engineers in 1842.

Between 1846 and 1848, Meade served in the Mexican War, for which he was promoted to first lieutenant for bravery at the Battle of Monterey. When he returned to the United States, Meade was assigned further civil projects, such as building lighthouses and breakwaters in Florida and New Jersey. He was promoted to captain in 1856. When the Civil War broke out, Meade was working on a surveying mission to the Great Lakes region.

Promoted to brigadier general of volunteers in August of 1861, Meade took command of the 2nd Brigade of the Pennsylvania Reserves and helped design the construction of defenses around Washington, DC. The brigade fought with McClellan's army during the Battle of Seven Days at which Meade suffered wounds to his arm, back, and side. He recovered in time to fight again at Second Bull Run. At the Battle of South Mountain he was given command of the 3rd Division, First Corps and fought bravely with his troops yet again.

Meade had established himself as a "fighting general," earning the respect of his troops and the officers above him. At the Battle of Antietam in September 1862, Meade took command of the First Corps when its commander, Joseph Hooker, was wounded. Meade was wounded again, this time in the thigh, during this battle. At Fredericksburg that December, Meade's division made the only breakthrough of the Confederate lines, attacking Lieutenant General "Stonewall" Jackson's corps. Promoted to major general and given command of Fifth Corps, Meade would fight again at Chancellorsville in May 1863.

In the pre-dawn hours of June 28, a special messenger reached Meade, who was encamped with the army near Frederick, Maryland. In a letter from Halleck, Meade was promoted to command the Army of the Potomac, with orders to confront Lee as he invaded Pennsylvania. Unknown to Meade at the time, that confrontation was only three days away.

Meade was an inspired choice by Lincoln.

In a plain little wall-tent, just like the rest, pen in hand, seated on a camp-stool and bending over a map, is the new "General Commanding" for the army of the Potomac. Tall, slender, not ungainly, but certainly not handsome or graceful, thin-faced, with grizzled beard and moustache, a broad and high but retreating forehead, from each corner of which the slightly-curling hair recedes, as if giving premonition of baldness—apparently between forty-five and fifty years of age—altogether a man who impresses you rather as a thoughtful student than as a dashing soldier—so General Meade looks in his tent.

—Whitelaw Reid

General Meade (seated at center) with generals on his command staff at Culpeper, Virginia, in September 1863. Gouverneur K. Warren is on the left. Photo credit: Library of Congress.

He was a proven combat leader, one without political ambitions, and Lincoln knew he could count on him to defend Pennsylvania from Lee's invasion. Where other generals had shown **timidity** in opposing Lee aggressively, Meade knew his duty was to seek battle.

On the night of June 30, he wrote his wife: "All is going on well. I think I have relieved Harrisburg and Philadelphia, and that Lee has now come to the conclusion that he must attend to other matters. I continue well, but much oppressed with a sense of responsibility and the magnitude of the great interests entrusted to me . . . Pray for me and **beseech** our heavenly Father to permit me to be an instrument to save my country and advance a just cause."

The battle at Gettysburg over the next three days was the crowning moment for Meade in a lifetime devoted to the service of his country. As a topographic engineer, Meade knew the importance of holding the key terrain on any battlefield. In the early hours of the fighting, Meade entrusted his best officers to lead in his stead and to make decisions that could win or lose the battle before he was even on the field. In this he was most ably served by Buford, Reynolds, and Hancock, who collectively saved the heights near Gettysburg from falling into Lee's hands.

Meade's great success on July 3, in defeating Pickett's Charge was quickly followed a few weeks later by what many considered his greatest failure. With the Potomac River flooded by heavy rain and his only pontoon bridge captured by Union cavalry, Lee was trapped on the northern bank, dug in behind fixed positions in front of Williamsport. Meade was cautious, though, and this time to a fault.

The caution and thoroughness he displayed at Gettysburg worked against him, faced off with Lee now on the defensive. Just miles away was Antietam where a year earlier, under very similar circumstances, Lee had fought tenaciously against a Union attack that became the single costliest day of fighting in American history. Surely this was on Meade's mind as he contemplated attacking at Williamsport.

With his most aggressive and able corps commander, Winfield Scott Hancock, wounded at Gettysburg, his remaining officers voted against attacking Lee at a council of war on the evening of July 12. Meade agreed to wait one more day until he had a proper **reconnaissance** of Lee's position. That same evening, Lee's engineers improvised a pontoon bridge and his army escaped over the Potomac. The old fox had slipped the noose.

Lincoln was anguished by the news. The president was quoted as saying, "We had them within our grasp. We had only to stretch forth our hands and they were ours. And nothing I could say or do could make the Army move."

Meade promptly and furiously offered his resignation from command. This gesture Lincoln quickly (and wisely) refused, instead offering his thanks for what was accomplished at Gettysburg. Meade's failure to prevent Lee's escape has been a point of debate ever since. Meade retained command of the Army of the Potomac and served under Ulysses S. Grant for the remainder of the war.

Meade continued in military and public service after the war as a commissioner of Fairmount Park in Philadelphia from 1866 until his death in 1872. The lighthouses he designed still stand as monuments to the life of peace he wished to pursue as a civil engineer.

Meade should be remembered as one of the great Civil War generals. He was one of the few combat leaders who appreciated changes in technology and tactics that made frontal assaults a tragic waste of human lives. The greatest compliment to Meade's abilities as an army commander came from Robert E. Lee. On the night of June 28, 1863, when Lee received word that Meade had been promoted to command the Union army, he told his fellow officers, "General Meade will commit no **blunder** in my front, and if I make one he will make haste to take advantage of it."

At Gettysburg, when the country needed a careful and thoughtful leader, Meade was there. His trust in his subordinates, his careful movement and deployment of vast numbers of men, guns, and supplies to Gettysburg, and his foresight in sensing Lee would attack his center line on July 3, were all marks of a great general. He was one of the few Union generals to face Robert E. Lee in open battle and to defeat him.

Gettysburg in 1863 taken from the Chambersburg Pike. Photo credit: Matthew Brady, Library of Congress.

J. E. B. STUART'S RIDE

On June 26, one day before crossing into Pennsylvania, General Lee told another officer, "We have again out-maneuvered the enemy, who even now don't know where we are or what are our designs. Our whole army will be in Pennsylvania the day after tomorrow leaving the enemy far behind, and obliged to follow us by forced marches. I hope with those advantages to accomplish some signal result, and to end the war if Providence favors us." A great battle awaited them somewhere north of the Shenandoah Valley, he said, pointing on the map in the vicinity of Gettysburg.

A few days earlier, on June 22, Lee had finalized his plan of advance with cavalry leader General Stuart. He ordered Stuart to use part of his five brigades to guard the mountain passes behind Lee's

> *He is commonly called Jeb Stuart, on account of his initials; he is a good-looking, jovial character, exactly like his photographs. He is a good and gallant soldier . . .*
>
> —Colonel Arthur James Lyon Fremantle

This is a town of some size and importance. All its houses were shut up; but the natives were in the streets, or at the upper windows, looking in a scowling and bewildered manner at the Confederate troops, who were marching gaily past to the tune of "Dixie Land." The women (many of whom were pretty and well dressed) were particularly sour and disagreeable in their remarks. I heard one of them say, "Look at Pharaoh's army going to the Red Sea." Others were pointing and laughing at Hood's ragged Jacks, who were passing at the time.

This division, well known for its fighting qualities, is composed of Texans, Alabamians, and Arkansans, and they certainly are a queer lot to look at. They carry less than any other troops; many of them have only got an old piece of carpet or rug as baggage; many have discarded their shoes in the mud; all are ragged and dirty, but full of good humor and confidence in themselves and in their general, Hood. They answered the numerous taunts of the Chambersburg ladies with cheers and laughter.

The Confederate soldiers were certainly in good spirits. The fruits of their invasion literally fell into their hands as captured **provisions** were plentiful. The men often joked that C.S.A. (Confederate States of America) actually meant corn, salt, and apples, which were the standard issues of their rations. Edward Alexander Moore, an artillerist in Longstreet's corps, wrote of their sudden change in diet: "I give the bill-of-fare of a breakfast my mess enjoyed while on this road: Real coffee and sugar, light bread, biscuits with lard in them, butter, apple-butter, a fine dish of fried chicken, and a quarter roast lamb!"

Longstreet's men encamped just outside Chambersburg alongside Hill's troops. Lee arrived the following day, Sunday, June 28, and established headquarters in a quite grove called Messersmith's Woods. Lieutenant William Owen, an artillery officer in Longstreet's command, described the scene: "The general has little of the pomp and circumstance of war about his person. A Confederate flag marks the whereabouts of his headquarters, which are here in a little enclosure of some couple of acres of timber. There are about half a dozen tents and as many baggage wagons and ambulances . . . Lee was evidently annoyed at the absence of Stuart and the cavalry, and asked several officers, myself among the number, if we knew anything of the whereabouts of Stuart. The eyes and ears of the army are evidently missing and are greatly needed by the commander."

A QUESTION OF SLAVERY

African American refugees fleeing north away from Lee's invasion. Illustrated by Rodney Thomson.

For the African American residents of Gettysburg, rumors of Lee's invasion were terrifying. If captured by the rebels they would likely be put in chains and returned to slavery. Elizabeth Salome "Sallie" Myers, a Gettysburg schoolteacher, wrote of their terrible plight: "Every report of raiding would set the Africans to migrating, they were so afraid they'd be carried off into slavery. They looked very ragged and forlorn, and some exaggerated their ills by pretending to be lame, for they wanted to appear as undesirable as possible to any beholder who might be tempted to take away their freedom."

A bank clerk from town remembered that "a great many refugees passed through Gettysburg going northward. Some would have a spring wagon and a horse, but usually they were on foot, burdened with bundles containing a couple of quilts, some clothing, and a few cooking utensils. . . . The farmers along the roads sheltered them nights. Most of these here poor runaways would drift into the towns and find employment, and there they'd make their future homes."

What these refugees lacked in material possessions they made up for with hope—hope for a future free of slavery. They dreamed of a place where their children would be educated and make a life for themselves; of controlling their own destinies. By 1863, Lincoln desired to provide that very future for them by ending slavery in America forever.

At the time of the start of the Civil War, over three million African Americans remained in chains in the South. Another million slaves lived in the **border states** that were still loyal to the Union. However, the war that began in 1861 was not fought to end slavery. The Confederate States of America were formed, in fact, to gain southern independence in reaction to an overpowering domination by northern political interests. Lincoln's sole purpose at the war's start was, as he wrote in a letter to Horace Greeley, the editor of the *New York Tribune* in August 1862, "to save the Union, and is not either to save or to destroy slavery." Lincoln felt he had no constitutional authority to **deprive** citizens of their property, including slaves, even in a war of rebellion.

But as the conflict dragged into its second year with no end in sight, Lincoln's opinion began to shift. He saw an opportunity, using the

First reading of the "Emancipation Proclamation" of President Lincoln painted by Francis Bicknell Carpenter. Image credit: White House Collection.

authority as Commander in Chief, to free the slaves of those states in rebellion; this would be a way to help win the war. On September 22, 1862, Lincoln issued a **proclamation** that he would order the **emancipation** of all slaves in any state of the Confederacy that did not return to Union control by January 1, 1863. He also began pushing for the passage of the Thirteenth Amendment to **abolish** slavery on American soil.

The Emancipation Proclamation redefined the war by making the abolition of slavery a primary goal for the Union. General de Trobriand summarized the effect: "It was no longer a question of the Union as it was, that was to be re-established, but the Union as it should be. That is to say, washed clean from its original sin. We were no longer merely the soldiers of a political controversy, we were now missionaries on a great work of **redemption**, the armed liberators of millions. The war was ennobled. The object was higher." As Lee advanced into Pennsylvania, the Army of the Potomac knew it could not suffer another defeat; it had to win.

Brigadier General James Régis de Trobriand.
Photo credit: Library of Congress.

LEE MOVES ON THE WORD OF A SPY

That night a mysterious stranger was brought to Longstreet's chief of staff, Lieutenant Colonel Moxley Sorrel: "At night I was roused by a detail of the provost guard bringing up a suspicious prisoner. I knew him instantly; it was Harrison, the scout, filthy and ragged . . . He had come to 'Report to the General, who was sure to be with the army,' and truly his report was long and valuable." The Federal army had crossed the Potomac three days ago and was far into Maryland. Harrison knew the locations of five of the enemy's seven army corps. Three were already at Frederick with two more marching north from Frederick toward South Mountain. He also brought news that General Meade had taken command of the army. This information was already twenty-four hours old.

Lee had not heard from Stuart for three days now. Stuart had never before failed him. But even now Lee was unaware of Stuart's location, and he had only the word of a paid spy on which to plan his next move. The time for action had come, though, and Lee did not hesitate. Sorrel noted, "It was on this, the report of a single scout, in the absence of cavalry, that the

Brigadier General John Buford.
Photo credit: Library of Congress.

army moved . . . [Lee] sent orders to bring Ewell immediately back from the North about Harrisburg, and join his left. Then he started A. P. Hill off at sunrise for Gettysburg, followed by Longstreet. The enemy was there, and there our General would strike him."

MEADE ORDERS THE FIRST CORPS TO GETTYSBURG

As Meade took command on June 28, intelligence on Lee's army became clearer. Spies in Hagerstown, Maryland, estimated the enemy's strength at 80,000 men and 275 cannons. Meade knew Lee had sent Ewell's corps north to York and Carlisle while Longstreet's and Hill's troops remained in the vicinity of Chambersburg. Orders were given to keep the Federal army marching northwest from Frederick to Taneytown, where Meade set up his headquarters. To screen the advance of the army, Brigadier General John Buford was ordered to take two brigades of cavalry into Gettysburg and defend the town if attacked.

Lee began moving his army east toward Gettysburg on Monday the 29th, with Hill's Third Corps camping in Cashtown for the night. Longstreet's First Corps would follow

"Battle Cry of Freedom"

Yes we'll rally round the flag, boys, we'll rally once again,

Shouting the battle cry of freedom,

We will rally from the hillside, we'll gather from the plain,

Shouting the battle cry of freedom!

(Chorus)

The Union forever! Hurrah, boys, hurrah!

Down with the traitor, up with the star;

While we rally round the flag, boys, rally once again,

Shouting the battle cry of freedom!

We are springing to the call of our brothers gone before,

Shouting the battle cry of freedom!

And we'll fill our vacant ranks with a million freemen more,

Shouting the battle cry of freedom!

(Chorus)

We will welcome to our numbers the loyal, true and brave,

Shouting the battle cry of freedom!

And although they may be poor, not a man shall be a slave,

Shouting the battle cry of freedom!

on the 30th as far as Greenwoood, and Ewell's Second Corps would march south from Carlisle. Major General Henry Heth, commanding the lead division of Hill's corps, ordered a brigade to Gettysburg on the 30th to find supplies, especially shoes, for his ill-equipped soldiers.

Thus, by Tuesday, June 30, the Union and Confederate armies were on a collision course toward Gettysburg. Meade had only been in command of his army for two days; his troops were stretched out along the roads from Frederick—hot and exhausted from hard marching. He was about to face the legendary Robert E. Lee in what could be the decisive battle of the war. Yet Meade did have one precious advantage over Lee—he knew where his enemy was, while Lee, without cavalry, was advancing blindly.

Daniel Skelly recalled the growing tension among the people of Gettysburg: "The 28th and 29th were exciting days in Gettysburg for we knew the Confederate army, or a part of it at least, was within a few miles of our town and at night we could see from the house-tops the campfires in the mountains eight miles west of us. We expected it to march into our town at any moment and we had no information as to the whereabouts of the Army of the Potomac."

BUFORD'S CAVALRY ENTERS GETTYSBURG

Tillie Pierce witnessed the arrival of the first Union soldiers at Gettysburg on Tuesday, June 30:

A great number of Union cavalry began to arrive in the town. They passed northwardly along Washington Street, turned toward the west on reaching Chambersburg Street, and passed out in the direction of the Theological Seminary.

It was to me a novel and grand sight. I had never seen so many soldiers at one time. They were Union soldiers and that was enough for me, for I then knew we had protection, and I felt they were our dearest friends. I afterwards learned that these men were Buford's cavalry, numbering about six thousand men.

A crowd of "us girls" were standing on the corner of Washington and High Streets as these soldiers passed by. Desiring to encourage them, who, as we were told, would before long be in battle, my sister started to sing the old war song "Our Union Forever." As some of us did not know the whole of the piece we kept repeating the chorus.

A little less than Tillie's estimate, Buford had just under 3,000 men in his command and a battery of six cannon. Daniel Skelly also watched on Chambersburg Street as thousands of cavalry rode through town and thought, "Surely now we were safe and the Confederate army would never reach Gettysburg . . . General Buford sat on his horse in the street in front of me, entirely alone,

Washington Street, Gettysburg, in 1863. Photo credit: Ken Giorlando.

facing to the west in profound thought . . . It was the only time I ever saw the general and his calm demeanor and soldierly appearance . . . made a deep impression on me."

General Buford was a West Point graduate and a veteran of the early fighting against the Sioux Indians in Texas. In 1862, Buford had fought at Second Bull Run and Antietam. At Brandy Station he commanded a division of cavalry against Stuart's troopers. His experience was about to prove invaluable over the next three days. As he moved his troopers into the open fields north of Gettysburg they encountered Confederate soldiers in Brigadier General

James Pettigrew's brigade sent to Gettysburg for supplies. Under strict orders not to bring on a fight, the rebels fell back to Cashtown and reported their discovery of Union cavalry occupying Gettysburg.

Buford sent scouts in all directions to locate and identify what enemy units were in front of him. He knew what was at stake. A half mile behind them, just outside the town, was a low ridgeline called Cemetery Hill. At each end of that ridge were larger hills: Culp's Hill to the north and two hills at the southern end named Little and Big Round Top. It was well known that in any battle, whoever controlled

Water for the marching troops.
Illustrated by Rodney Thomson.

the high ground possessed a great advantage over an attacking force. Buford knew he had to delay Lee's army long enough for the Union infantry to **reinforce** him and protect those heights, so he **deployed** his men in a series of two defensive lines centered along a wooded hill north of Gettysburg named McPherson's Ridge.

At 10:30 PM he sent a message to Major General John F. Reynolds, who commanded three of the infantry corps that were approaching Gettysburg from the east. He reported that Hill's entire corps was at Cashtown, nine miles away to the west. Enemy **pickets** were in sight of his own along the Chambersburg Pike. Longstreet's corps was behind Hill's, perhaps by a day's march.

It was a gala day. The people were out in force, and in their Sunday attire to welcome the troopers in blue. The church bells rang out a joyous peal, and dense masses of beaming faces filled the streets, as the narrow column of fours threaded its way through their midst. Lines of men stood on either side, with pails of water or apple-butter, and passed a "sandwich" to each soldier as he passed. At intervals of a few feet, were bevies of women and girls, who handed up bouquets and wreaths of flowers. By the time the center of the town was reached, every man had a bunch of flowers in his hand, or a wreath around his neck . . . The people were overjoyed, and received us with an enthusiasm and a hospitality born of full hearts.

—Colonel J. H. Kidd, 6th Michigan Cavalry

Major General John Fulton Reynolds. Photo credit: Reynolds family papers, Franklin & Marshall College.

A captured enemy **courier** told him that Ewell's corps was advancing toward Gettysburg from Carlisle from the north.

Buford knew that by morning he would face an entire rebel corps of 25,000 men. By all accounts, Buford saw that Lee was concentrating his whole army at Gettysburg. If Ewell's corps made it to the town by the next day, two thirds of Lee's army—50,000 soldiers—would advance against whatever Union forces could reach Gettysburg in time. When one of his brigade commanders spoke confidently of whipping any rebels the next day, Buford said, "No, you won't. They will attack you in the morning; and they will come 'booming'—**skirmishers** three deep. You will have to fight like the devil to hold your own until supports arrive."

Reading Buford's report Meade sent orders for Reynolds to advance his First Corps to

The McPherson Farm photographed just after the battle in 1863. Photo credit: Matthew Brady, Library of Congress.

Gettysburg in the morning with the Eleventh and Third Corps to follow. Reynolds was given command authority to act in Meade's stead on the battlefield should there be action the next day. Meade would remain at Taneytown—fourteen miles from Gettysburg—to stay at the center of his army as events developed. Meade's objective, in sending Reynolds to Gettysburg, was to force Lee into attacking his army on ground of his own choosing.

At Cashtown, Hill listened

Major General Henry Heth

with disbelief that his troops had encountered Federal cavalry at Gettysburg. Brigadier General James Pettigrew insisted they had tangled with Union troopers before withdrawing. Hill believed his subordinate officer had only encountered local militia, as he had just been informed by Lee that the closest Union troops were near Middleburg, Maryland, several days away. General Heth asked his corps commander if he had any objections to advancing his division to Gettysburg in the morning. Hill replied, "None in the world."

> *All is going on well. I think I have relieved Harrisburg and Philadelphia, and that Lee has now come to the conclusion that he must attend to other matters. I continue well, but much oppressed with a sense of responsibility and the magnitude of the great interests entrusted to me ... Pray for me and beseech our heavenly Father to permit me to be an instrument to save my country and advance a just cause.*
>
> —George Gordon Meade

Chapter Three

Wednesday, July 1, 1863

Blessed be the LORD my strength,
which teacheth my hands to war,
and my fingers to fight:

Bow thy heavens, O Lord, and come down:
touch the mountains, and they shall
smoke.

—Psalm 144:5

Dawn welcomed a perfect summer's morning that promised heat and humidity to follow. At 7:00 AM Buford's pickets saw a dust cloud over the Chambersburg Pike made by advancing rebel infantry. Heth was approaching Gettysburg with his entire division and its artillery. Skirmishers engaged each other while Heth ordered his artillery to open fire and scare off the "militia" opposing him behind the wood fences along Herr's Ridge. Yet Buford's men were armed with fast-loading carbine rifles and the dismounted cavalrymen put up a tough fight.

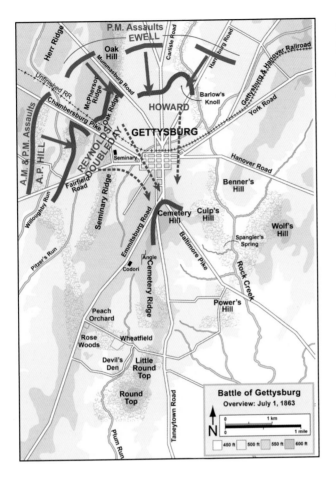

Map by Hal Jespersen, www.cwmaps.com.

Realizing he had encountered more than just local militia, Heth ordered two of his brigades forward in force. Buford's skillful deployment of his defenses forced Heth to take ninety minutes to deploy the two brigades into a line of battle. As the Confederates advanced, Buford's skirmishers fell back to McPherson's Ridge, where they joined the main line of defense.

It was now 9:00 AM. Heth surveyed the Union defenses from Herr's Ridge and made a fateful decision. Instead of obeying Lee's orders

not to bring on a major battle, he ordered two brigades forward to occupy Gettysburg. General Archer's Brigade advanced to the right of the Chambersburg Pike and General Davis's on the left. The fight was on.

Daniel Skelly was more than a witness to these first hours of fighting. Upon hearing that Confederate troops were coming down the Chambersburg Pike, he and a friend ran toward the Union lines to see what they could see:

> *I went directly across the fields to Seminary Ridge . . . just where the old . . . railroad cut through it. The ridge was full of men and boys from town, all eager to witness a brush with the Confederates and not dreaming of the terrible conflict that was to occur on that day and not having the slightest conception of the proximity of the two armies.*
>
> *I climbed up a good-sized oak tree so as to have a good view of the ridge west and northwest of us, where the two brigades of cavalry were then being placed. We could then hear distinctly the skirmish fire in the vicinity of Marsh Creek, about three miles from our position and could tell that it was approaching nearer and nearer as our skirmishers fell back slowly toward the town contesting every inch of ground. We could see clearly on the ridge . . . the formation of the line of battle of Buford's Cavalry, which had dismounted, some of the men taking*

McPherson's Ridge—July 1, 1863. Thirty-seven-year-old Union cavalry General John Buford sits astride his horse beside the McPherson barn and directs Calef's battery into position. The Union troops held their line against the advancing Confederates until re-enforcements arrived, holding their position in the climatic battle known as McPherson's Ridge. Illustrated by Don Troiani.

charge of the horses and the others forming a line of battle, acting as infantry.

Nearer and nearer came the skirmish line as it fell back before the advancing Confederates, until at last the line on the ridge beyond became engaged. Soon the artillery opened fire and shot and shell began to fly over our heads, one of them passing dangerously near the top of the tree I was on. There was a general stampede toward town and I quickly slipped down from my perch and joined the retreat to the rear of our gallant men and boys . . . a cannon ball struck the earth about fifteen or twenty feet from me, scattering the ground somewhat about me and quickening my pace considerably.

For God Sake Forward—July 1, 1863. The fearless men of the 2nd Wisconsin (Iron Brigade), lead by General John F. Reynolds, rush into the grove of trees on McPherson's Ridge to stem the advancing Confederates during the opening encounters at Gettysburg. Illustrated by Don Troiani.

THE ARRIVAL OF MAJOR GENERAL JOHN REYNOLDS AND THE FIRST CORPS

That morning, riding ahead of his First Corps only a few miles from Gettysburg, Major General Reynolds and his staff received a message from Buford that his cavalry were heavily engaged by enemy infantry. Upon receiving this news, Reynolds instantly sent word to General Wadsworth of the First Corps to "close up and come on" as other riders raced to inform General Howard of the Eleventh Corps and General Sickles of the Third to advance with all haste to Gettysburg.

Galloping ahead, Reynolds met Buford coming down from his observation post in the **cupola** of the Gettysburg Seminary College. Together they rode onto McPherson's Ridge just after

10:00 AM, where the line of troopers desperately held on against nearly 3,000 Confederates. Amid the deafening roar of gunfire Reynolds yelled to Buford, "Can you hold until my corps arrives?"

"I reckon I can!" Buford yelled back.

Reynolds turned to a junior officer and ordered: "Ride at your utmost speed to General Meade. Tell him the enemy are advancing in strong force, and that I fear they will get to the heights beyond the town before I can. I will fight them inch by inch, and if driven into the town, I will barricade the streets and hold them back as long as possible. Don't spare your horse . . ."

A few minutes later, Reynolds rode south down the Emmitsburg Road to meet Brigadier General James Wadsworth's 1st Division of the First Corps, who were just arriving. Reynolds ordered them to tear down fences and advance directly to the line of battle across the fields. Colonel Rufus Dawes and his 6th Wisconsin Regiment of the Iron Brigade were among these units. Dawes remembered: "To make a show in the streets of Gettysburg, I brought our drum corps to the front and had the colors unfurled. The drum major . . . had begun to play 'The Campbell's are Coming,' and the regiment had closed its ranks and swung into the step, when we first heard the cannon of the enemy, firing on the cavalry of General Buford. The troops ahead turned across the fields to the left of Gettysburg, toward the Seminary Ridge."

Reynolds personally deployed his first two brigades and a battery of artillery along McPherson's Ridge. Brigadier General Solomon Meredeth's Iron Brigade defended McPherson's Woods west of the Cashtown Pike, and Brigadier General Lysander Cutler's brigade arrayed for battle to the east by the **railway cut**. The Union troops formed a line just as Heth's two Confederate brigades reached the Federal positions. Suddenly reinforced by infantry, Buford's cavalry troopers could now outmatch the advancing Confederates. The opposing lines came upon each other suddenly and the fighting exploded into a murderous exchange of volleys at short range.

Reynolds advanced with the Second Wisconsin, deploying them into the trees along McPherson's Ridge, which were filled with Confederate soldiers of Archer's brigade. Reynolds yelled to his men above the battle, "Forward men, forward for God's sake and drive those fellows out of those woods!" At that moment, an enemy bullet struck Reynolds in the head, killing him instantly. Though he commanded the field for only an hour, Reynolds committed the First and Eleventh corps to battle, rescued Buford's two brigades from annihilation, and saved the high ground south of Gettysburg from falling into Lee's hands. Command of the First Corps now fell to 2nd Division commander, Major General Abner Doubleday.

As the armies collided the action became divided by the Chambersburg Pike. Archer's brigade had advanced south of the road over Willoughby Run toward the Herbst farm and straight into a devastating ambush by units of the Iron Brigade. A cry went up along the Confederate line: "Yanks! It's them damned 'Black Hats' again!" Caught in the open and without support, nearly the entire brigade was shot down or forced to surrender.

North of the road, Davis's brigade was overwhelming Cutler's defenders. As the Federals retreated Colonel Dawes's 6th Wisconsin and two New York regiments were ordered into action to assist Cutler's Brigade. Dawes recounted the moment:

The regiment halted at the fence along the Cashtown Turnpike, a long line of yelling Confederates could be seen running forward and firing, and our troops of Cutler's brigade were running back in disorder. The fire of our carefully aimed muskets, resting on the fence rails, striking their flank, soon checked the rebels in their headlong pursuit. The rebel line swayed and bent, and suddenly stopped firing and the men ran into the railroad cut, parallel to the Cashtown Turnpike. I ordered my men to climb over the turnpike fences and advance . . .

When over the fences and in the field, and subjected to an infernal fire, I first saw the 95th New York regiment coming

The Fall of Reynolds depicted by Alfred Rudolph Waud. Image credit: Library of Congress.

Fight for The Colors—July 1, 1863. The Iron Brigade's 6th Wisconsin dashed gallantly forward toward the 2nd Mississippi. The hand-to-hand struggle for the flag of the 2nd Mississippi was one of the most heroic moments of the first day's conflict at Gettysburg. Illustrated by Don Troiani.

gallantly into line upon our left . . . Major Edward Pye appeared to be in command. . . . Running to the major, I said, "We must charge." The gallant major replied, "Charge it is." . . . We were receiving a fearfully destructive fire from the hidden enemy. Men who had been shot were leaving the ranks in crowds. With the colors at the advance point, the regiment firmly and hurriedly moved forward,

while the whole field behind streamed with men who had been shot, and who were struggling to the rear or sinking in death upon the ground.

The only commands I gave, as we advanced, were, "Align on the colors! Close up on the colors! Close up on the colors!" The regiment was being so broken up that this order alone could hold the body together. Meanwhile the colors fell upon the ground several times but were raised again by the heroes of the color guard. Four hundred and twenty men started in the regiment from the turnpike fence, of whom about two hundred and forty reached the railroad cut.

My notice that we were upon the enemy, was a general cry from our men of: "Throw down your muskets! Down with your muskets!" Running forward through our line of men, I found myself face to face with hundreds of rebels, whom I looked down upon in the railroad cut, which was, where I stood, four feet deep . . . I shouted: "Where is the colonel of this regiment?" An officer in gray, with stars on his collar, who stood among the men in the cut, said: "Who are you?" I said: "I command this regiment. Surrender or I will fire." The

officer replied not a word, but promptly handed me his sword, and his men, who still held them, threw down their muskets . . . Corporal Frank Asbury Waller brought me the captured battle flag. It was the flag of the 2nd Mississippi Volunteers, one of the oldest and most distinguished regiments in the Confederate army. It belonged to the brigade commanded by Joseph R. Davis, the nephew of Jefferson Davis.

TILLIE PIERCE LEAVES FOR JACOB WEIKERT'S FARM

As the fighting north of town grew into a thunder of musketry and cannon fire, the people of Gettysburg realized their town might soon become a battlefield. Tillie Pierce recalled her growing fears that morning:

The Jacob Weikert farm as it appears today. Photo credit: The Gettysburg Daily.

It was between nine and ten o'clock when we first noticed firing in the direction of Seminary Ridge. At first the sound was faint, then it grew louder. Soon the booming of cannon was heard, then great clouds of smoke were seen rising beyond the ridge. The sound became louder and louder, and was now incessant. The troops passing us moved faster, the men had now become excited and urged on their horses. The battle was waging.

Our neighbor, Mrs. Schriver, called at the house and said she would leave the town and go to her father's (Jacob Weikert), who lived on the Taneytown road at the eastern slope of the Round Top.

Mr. Schriver, her husband, was then serving in the Union army, so that under all the circumstances at this time surrounding her, Mrs. Schriver did not feel safe in the house . . . she thought it safer for herself and two children to go to her parents, who lived about three miles to the south. She requested that I be permitted to accompany her, and as it was regarded a safer place for me than to remain in town, my parents readily consented that I should go.

About one o'clock we started on foot; the battle still going on. We proceeded out Baltimore Street and entered the Evergreen Cemetery. This was our easiest and most direct route, as it would bring us to the Taneytown road a little further on. As we were passing along the Cemetery hill, our men were already planting cannon. They told us to hurry as fast as possible; that we were in great danger of being shot by the Rebels, whom they expected would shell toward us at any moment. We fairly ran to get out of this new danger.

At last we reached Mr. Weikert's and were gladly welcomed to their home. It was not long after our arrival, until Union artillery came hurrying by. It was indeed a thrilling sight. How the men impelled their horses! How the officers urged the men as they all flew past toward the sound of the battle!

After the artillery had passed, infantry began coming. I soon saw that these men were very thirsty and would go to the spring which is on the north side of the house.

I was not long in learning what I could do. Obtaining a bucket, I hastened to the spring, and there, with others, carried water to the moving column until the spring was empty. We then went to the pump standing on the south side of the house, and supplied water from it. Thus we continued giving water to our tired soldiers until night came on, when we sought rest indoors.

MEADE CALLS UPON HIS FINEST— MAJOR GENERAL WINFIELD SCOTT HANCOCK

Meade learned of the early fighting at Gettysburg while still at his Taneytown headquarters via messages from both Buford and Reynolds at 11:30 AM. Still hoping to fight on defensive terrain of his choosing along a position near Pike's Creek, he did not yet commit his entire army to Gettysburg. Instead, Meade ordered Major General Winfield Scott Hancock to advance the Second Corps up the Taneytown Road toward Gettysburg to cover an avenue of retreat for the First Corps should Reynolds decide to withdraw.

Major General Winfield Scott Hancock.
Photo credit: Library of Congress.

Major General Oliver Otis Howard.
Photo credit: Library of Congress.

By 1:00 PM Meade learned of Reynolds's death and that Major General Otis Howard was now in command on the field. Meade did not think much of General Howard's leadership, for at Chancellorsville, it was Howard's Eleventh Corps that had broken under Stonewall Jackson's flank attack. So Meade rode to General Hancock's headquarters with orders for him to ride toward Gettysburg with authority to decide if the town would indeed be the location to make a united stand against Lee. The time was 1:30 PM.

LEE MOVES TO THE BATTLEFIELD

General Lee advanced toward Cashtown accompanied by Longstreet, his senior advisor. Leaving Greenwood that morning, neither Lee nor any of his generals expected to encounter the Union army that day. Without Stuart's cavalry to warn him, Lee was unaware that Buford's two brigades had arrived in Gettysburg the day before, or that the Union's First Corps was encamped eight miles from the town. His first clue that trouble lay ahead came with the faint sound of cannon fire as he passed through the Cashtown Gap. He quickly rode to Cashtown and sought Hill at his headquarters.

General Hill was about to set out for Gettysburg when Lee approached him. Just after noon a staff officer arrived, informing Lee that Ewell was advancing with the Second Corps to Gettysburg. Lee sent a reply ordering Ewell to avoid a general engagement. Lee wished to avoid a major battle until all of his three corps were assembled. Impatient at the lack of information and hearing no end to the gunfire, Lee mounted Traveller and rode toward the sound of the guns, intent on taking command of whatever battle lay ahead.

EWELL ATTACKS THE UNION RIGHT

After narrowly escaping with his life that morning, Daniel Skelly was still determined to see what was happening on the battlefield:

Being anxious to see more of the battle, I concluded I would go up upon the observatory on the store building of the Fahnestock Brothers, situated on the northwest corner of Baltimore and West Middle Streets, and just across the street from the court house. The observatory . . . had a good view of the field where the battle was then being fought.

We had been up there quite a little time when I observed a general and his staff coming down Baltimore Street from the south of the town. Upon reaching the court house, they halted and made an attempt to get up into the belfry to make observations, but they were unable to accomplish this. I went down into the street and going over to

met with fierce resistance, the weight of a full division would soon be applied on the exposed Union right—and it would have to crumble.

Major General John Gordon's brigade of Jubal Early's division led the attack on Blocher's Knoll in the renewed attack. He recalled, "With a ringing yell, my command rushed upon the line posted to protect the Union right. Here occurred a hand-to-hand struggle. That protecting Union line once broken left my command not only on the right flank but obliquely in rear of it. Any troops that were ever marshaled would, under like conditions, have been as surely and swiftly shattered. There was no alternative for Howard's men except to break and fly or to throw down their arms and surrender."

LEE ARRIVES ON THE BATTLEFIELD, 2:30 PM

Lee arrived in Gettysburg on a small rise of ground called Belmont Ridge next to the Chambersburg Pike that afternoon. He met with Hill and they observed the battle already underway as Union and Confederate artillery dueled across the open plain. To the north, three of General Ewell's brigades were engaging the Union line around Blocher's Knoll. Heth arrived and asked if he could renew the attack with his full division. Lee replied, "I do not wish to bring on a general engagement today. Longstreet is not up." Heth was sent back to his division to await events as Lee continued to observe Ewell's attack.

Stuart was on a useless, showy parade almost under the guns of the Washington forts . . .

When he rejoined Lee it was with exhausted horses and half worn-out men in the closing hours of Gettysburg.

Had he been with Lee where would our commander have made his battle? Possibly, not on that unfavorable ground of Gettysburg. Lee with his personally weak opponent, and Stuart by him, could almost have chosen the spot where he would be sure to defeat the Union Army.

—Lieutenant Colonel Moxley Sorrel

John Burns, the "Old Patriot" of Gettysburg.
Photo credit: Timothy H. O'Sullivan, Library of Congress.

THE "OLD PATRIOT"

As the Union army prepared for the renewed Confederate attack along McPherson's Ridge, an officer was approached by an odd-looking old man. He was wearing a long frock coat and a felt hat, and was carrying a flintlock musket and a pocket full of ammunition. This was John Burns, age sixty-nine, a veteran of the War of 1812, and a retired constable of Gettysburg—something of a **cantankerous** town character. He told the officer he wanted to fight. Told to join the "Wisconsin fellers," Burns fell in among the blue clad soldiers and blazed away with his antique weapon at the advancing rebels. Clipped by three bullets and taking one to the leg, his short military career ended, but John Burns survived his wounds to become a national hero. When President Lincoln visited Gettysburg later that November, he made it a point to visit with the "Old Patriot."

Here was the opportunity Lee had been looking for upon entering Pennsylvania. He knew the Union army was marching great distances in very hot weather to meet his army in battle. Lee intended to overwhelm any Union advance he encountered by massing his army against them, forcing them to retreat. In this way he could outnumber and destroy one Union corps after another and achieve an overwhelming victory. Yet the events of this day were by chance, not design, and without Stuart's help, Lee had no knowledge of which enemy forces were behind the two corps already at Gettysburg. Nor did Lee know the exact layout of the terrain past the town until the battle was already underway.

Just then a staff officer from Stuart's cavalry arrived. At last, there was word that Stuart's forces were thirty miles away, heading toward Carlisle and trying to link up with Ewell's corps. Lee sent the officer back to Stuart with orders to ride for Gettysburg at once. When Stuart and his troopers finally arrived the next afternoon, exhausted and dirty with only some captured wagons to boast of, Lee welcomed his wayward cavalryman with an icy glare: "Well, General, you are here at last."

Watching a division of Ewell's under the command of Jubal Early advance against Blocher's Knoll to the north, Heth returned to Lee and again requested that his division be allowed to attack. Knowing his forces were in a position to carry the day even without Longstreet's support, Lee approved. Within the hour, Heth advanced two fresh brigades against the Union's Iron Brigade at McPherson's Ridge and forced them back toward the town.

> *The failure to crush the Federal army in Pennsylvania in 1863, in the opinion of almost all of the officers of the Army of Northern Virginia, can be expressed in five words—the absence of the cavalry.*
> —Major General Henry Heth

Boy Colonel—July 1, 1863. The Confederacy's youngest Colonel, twenty-one-year-old Henry King Burgwyn Jr., commander of the 26th North Carolina, raised his sword as the troops pressed forward to drive the Northerners out of Gettysburg's Herr Ridge. Illustrated by Don Troiani.

The 26th North Carolina vs. the 24th Michigan

Among the attacking Confederate units was the 26th North Carolina regiment of Pettigrew's brigade, with 843 men. Led by the twenty-one-year-old "boy general" Colonel Henry K. Burgwyn, the 26th North Carolina was the largest regiment in either army at Gettysburg. Forced to advance over open terrain, across Willoughby's Run, against the Iron Brigade's 24th Michigan regiment under Colonel Henry A. Morrow (who was deployed in the Herbst Woods along McPherson's Ridge), the Confederate attack was quickly bloodied. As the Tarheels reached the woods, the two enemies stood only forty yards apart, firing volley after volley into each other's ranks until finally the Union soldiers were forced to withdraw. Private William Cheek described the fateful moments:

Colonel Henry King Burgwyn Jr.

Colonel Henry A. Morrow

Our regiment had been formed in line of battle and advanced a considerable distance towards the Federal lines. Our colors were very prominent in the center. Time after time they were shot down by the hot fire of infantry and artillery, and in all they fell fifteen times, sometimes the staff being broken and sometimes a color-bearer being shot down.

The color-sergeant was killed quite early in the advance and then a private of F company took the flag. He was shot once, but rose and went on, saying,

"Come on, boys!" and as the words left his lips was again shot down, when the flag was taken by Captain McCreary, who was killed a moment or two later.

Then Colonel Burgwyn himself took the colors and as we were advancing over the brow of a little hill and he was a few feet in advance of the center of the regiment, he was shot as he partly turned to give an order, a bullet passing through his abdomen. He fell backwards, the regiment continuing its advance, Lieutenant Colonel John R. Lane taking command and at the same time taking the flag from Colonel Burgwyn. In a moment, it seemed, he was shot, and then Captain W. S. Brewer, of my company, took the flag and carried it through the remainder of the advance, Major John Jones having then assumed command of the regiment.

By the end of the day's fighting the 26th North Carolina has lost over 500 men—killed, wounded, or missing. The unit would fight again on July 3, in Pickett's Charge, and finish the battle suffering 687 total casualties. The 24th Michigan lost 363 of their 496 men by the end of the fighting on July 3. Numerically, each of these proud regiments lost more than any other during the Battle of Gettysburg.

The Iron Brigade—July 1, 1863. The 24th Regiment Michigan Volunteers, led by Col. Henry A. Morrow, fights a desperate rear guard action near the Lutheran Seminary at Gettysburg. After numerous color bearers had been shot down, Col. Morrow raised the battle flag to encourage his men until he was grazed by a bullet in the head. Illustrated by Don Troiani.

Among the wounded during this attack was Major General Henry Heth, struck in the head by an enemy bullet. His life was spared by some rolled up newspaper he used in the brim of his hat to fit it snugly on his head. The folded papers were just enough to deflect the bullet, knocking the general unconscious for twenty-four hours and out of his command at Gettysburg. Brigadier General James Johnston Pettigrew would take command of Heth's division for Pickett's Charge on July 3.

THE FIRST CORPS WITHDRAWS TO SEMINARY RIDGE

Crushed from two directions, the Union lines were quickly outflanked on both ends of the field. The fighting at Blocher's Knoll and at McPherson's Woods was merciless and often at ranges as close as twenty paces.

General Doubleday, now commanding the First Corps, ordered his men to fall back to Seminary Ridge before they were overwhelmed. The Iron Brigade made a fighting retreat, contesting every inch of ground as they fell back. To the north, Howard's Eleventh Corps was also forced back in disarray less than an hour into the fight. All hope of saving the day now rested on the defense of a new line along Seminary Ridge, just in front of the college building near town. Colonel Rufus Dawes recalled the withdrawal:

*Major General Abner Doubleday.
Photo credit: Library of Congress.*

Under pressure of the battle, the whole line of Union troops fell back to the Seminary Ridge. I could plainly see the entire movement . . .

The enemy advanced so that the low ground between us and the Seminary Ridge in our rear was swept by their fire. It would cost many lives to march in line of battle through this fire.

I adopted the tactics of the rebels earlier in the day, and ordered my men to run into the railroad cut. Then instructing the men to follow in single file, I led the way, as fast as I could run, from this cut to the cut in the Seminary Ridge. About a cart load of dirt was ploughed over us by the rebel shell, but otherwise not a man was struck.

The ranks were promptly reformed, and we marched in the woods on the Seminary Ridge to the same position from which we had advanced. The whole first army corps was now in line of battle on the Seminary Ridge, and here that grand body of veteran soldiers made a heroic effort to stay the over-whelming tide that swept against them.

The Townspeople Help the Wounded

Daniel Skelly ran into the streets where the townspeople were busy doing whatever they could to help the wounded soldiers who were pouring into Gettysburg from the battlefield:

I walked down to our Centre Square and there met my mother carrying two buckets of water, looking for one of the improvised hospitals, to give it to the wounded . . .

We went down Carlisle Street to the McCurdy warehouse, just below the railroad, where the wounded were being brought in . . . No provision had yet been made for their care in the town and they were laid on the floor. We remained there quite a while giving them water and do-ing what we could for their relief . . .

As the afternoon wore away the churches and warehouses on Chambers-burg, Carlisle, and York Streets near-est the line of battle, were filled with wounded. Then the court house, as well as the Catholic, Presbyterian and Re-formed churches and the school house in High Street received the injured soldiers, until those places had reached their ca-pacity, when private homes were uti-lized, citizens volunteering to take them in and care for them.

The Fall of Seminary Ridge

In a grove before the Lutheran Seminary the survivors of the Iron Brigade and two other Pennsylvania brigades made a final stand behind a wood-and-stone fence. Heth now advanced two fresh brigades of North and South Carolin-ians to break the Union line. Rufus Dawes and his 6th Wisconsin were at the center of this action, as Dawes relates:

Battery "B," 4th U.S. artillery, under command of Lieutenant James Stew-art, came up, and General Wadsworth directed me to support it with my regiment . . . And now came the grand advance of the enemy . . . Along the

Seminary Ridge, flat upon their bellies, lay mixed together in one line of battle, the "Iron Brigade" and Roy Stone's "Bucktails." For a mile up and down the open friends in front, the splendid lines of the veterans of the Army of Northern Virginia swept down upon us. Their bearing was magnificent. They maintained their alignments with great precision.

Stewart fired shell until they appeared on the ridge east of Willoughby Run; when on this ridge they came forward with a rush. The musketry burst from the Seminary Ridge, every shot fired with care, and Stewart's men, with the regularity of a machine, worked their guns upon the enemy. The rebels came half way down the opposite slope, wavered, began to fire, then to scatter and then to run, and how our men did yell, "Come on, Johnny! come on!" Falling back over the ridge they came on again more cautiously, and pouring upon us from the start a deadly fire of deadly musketry. This killed Stewart's men and horses in great numbers, but did not seem to check his fire.

Lieutenant Clayton E. Rogers, aide on General Wadsworth's staff, came riding rapidly to me. Leaning over from his horse, he said very quietly: "The orders, colonel, are to retreat beyond the town. Hold your men together." I was astonished. The cheers of defiance along the line of the first corps, on Seminary Ridge, had scarcely died away. But a glace over the field to our right and rear was sufficient. There the troops of the eleventh corps appeared in full retreat, and long lines of Confederates, with fluttering banners and shining steel, were sweeping forward in pursuit of them without let or hindrance. It was a close race which could reach Gettysburg first, ourselves, or the rebel troops of Ewell's corps, who pursued our eleventh corps . . .

The weather was sultry. The sweat streamed from the faces of the men. There was not a drop of water in the canteens, and there had been none for hours. The streets were jammed with crowds of retreating soldiers, and with ambulances, artillery, and wagons. The cellars were crowded with men, sound in body, but craven in spirit, who had gone there to surrender . . . The rebels began to fire on us from houses and cross-lots .. . and the men returned their fire, shooting wherever the enemy appeared. It cleared the street of stragglers in short order. The way being open I marched again toward the Cemetery Hill.

We hurried along, not knowing certainly that we might not be marching into the clutches of the enemy. But the colors of the Union, floating over a well ordered line of men in blue, who were arrayed along the slope of Cemetery

Hill, became visible . . . With swifter steps we now pressed on up the hill, and, passing in through the ranks open to receive us, officers and men threw themselves in a state of almost perfect exhaustion on the green grass and the graves of the cemetery.

THE RETREAT THROUGH TOWN

Not all the regiments who fought that day were as well led or as lucky as the 6th Wisconsin. As the Eleventh Corps retreated through Gettysburg, units scattered and it became every man for himself in a vicious, close quarters street fight. Hundreds of Union soldiers were taken prisoner by the advancing Confederates. Trapped by the violence, the townspeople took shelter in the cellars of their homes.

Elizabeth Salome "Sallie" Myers was a twenty-one-year-old schoolteacher who lived in Gettysburg. As Union batteries and soldiers began retreating through the town she realized the coming danger. Union officers rode through the streets to warn the people to seek shelter. Elizabeth remembered the moment:

Then came the order: "Women and children to the cellars; the rebels will shell the town." We lost little time in obeying the order. My home was on West High Street, near Washington Street, and in the direct path of the retreat. From four to six we were in the cellar and those two hours I can never forget . . .

The noise above our heads, the rattling of musketry, the screeching of shells, and the unearthly yells, added to the cries of the children, were enough to shake the stoutest heart. After the rebels had gained full possession of the town, some of our men who had been captured were standing near the cellar window. One of them asked if some of us would take their addresses and the addresses of friends and write to them of their capture. I took thirteen and wrote as they requested . . . While the battle lasted we concealed and fed three men in our cellar.

GENERAL HANCOCK ARRIVES ON CEMETERY HILL

Colonel Fremantle arrived in time to witness the fall of Seminary Ridge: "At 4.30 PM we came in sight of Gettysburg, and joined General Lee and General Hill, who were on the top of one of the ridges which form the peculiar feature of the country around Gettysburg. We could see the enemy retreating up one of the opposite ridges, pursued by the Confederates with loud yells. The position into which the enemy had been driven was evidently a strong one. His right appeared to rest on a cemetery, on the top of a high ridge to the right of Gettysburg, as we looked at it."

Indeed, the Union forces had fallen back to a position of strength. What Fremantle and Lee saw was a brigade occupying Cemetery Hill,

Cemetery Hill—July 1, 1863. The celebrated General Winfield Scott Hancock is seen directing Major General A. Double-day to send his troops to secure Culp's Hill as the embattled Major General Oliver O. Howard looks on. Around them the troops of dozens of splintered commands begin to rally. Illustrated by Don Troiani.

which had been placed there that afternoon in reserve. The ridgeline was heavily defended by cannon and by 5:00 PM another 7,000 men from the Union First and Eleventh corps fell back to the ridge, adding to its defense. Unknown to Lee, the Union position was also being superbly led by General Hancock, who arrived about 4:30 PM just as the retreating soldiers reached Cemetery Hill.

Hancock's stern presence restored order to the exhausted and **demoralized** survivors of the day's fighting. Hancock knew that Cemetery Hill was the key position to fight a defensive battle. At 5:25 PM he sent a message to Mead: "We can fight here as the ground appears not unfavorable with good troops."

Holding Cemetery Hill was a victory for the Union, but with a very high price. General

Reynolds and almost a thousand of his men were dead. Four-and-a-half thousand more lay wounded on the field and thousands more taken prisoner. Yet as the hours went by, the Union position became stronger. As the survivors rallied around Hancock, more regiments began to arrive in a continuous stream to take their places along the line. While the Confederates had routed and nearly destroyed two Union corps that day, unless the Army of the Potomac withdrew, the battle was not over. Meade, now informed that his army was in a good defensive position at Gettysburg, intended to fight.

CULP'S HILL AND THE GHOST OF STONEWALL JACKSON

Lee and Longstreet viewed the Union position along Cemetery Hill from Seminary Ridge. Lee knew that the Confederates had won the day,

Major General Jubal Anderson Early

but a complete victory could not be claimed until the Union forces were driven from the high ground. Lee sent a message to Ewell "to carry the hill occupied by the enemy, if he found it **practicable**, but to avoid a general engagement until the arrival of the other divisions of the army." In other words, Ewell was to take the enemy position if he could without bringing on a larger battle than his corps could handle.

Ewell had two brigades he could advance against Cemetery Hill, but the position was being fortified and supported by Union artillery. He wisely concluded that such an attack could not succeed without support. He sent a message to Lee that he would advance if Lee would support him with additional forces to his right.

Upon receiving Ewell's message, Lee inquired how close the first division of Longstreet's corps was to Gettysburg. They were six miles away. It was now after 5:00 PM and darkness would fall before Longstreet's men could be in position. Lee replied to Ewell that "he regretted that his people were not up to support him on the right, but he wished him to take the Cemetery hill if it were possible." Lee had several brigades available but chose to keep them in reserve. Unsure of the force opposing him, Lee did not want to risk an all-out attack.

Knowing that an unsupported attack on the Union defenses would fail, Ewell quickly identified another objective. Eight hundred yards to the east of Cemetery Hill was Culp's Hill. If occupied, any artillery placed there could fire down upon the Union line along Cemetery Ridge and force its evacuation. The Army of the Potomac would be forced to leave Gettysburg.

It was, therefore, a key piece of terrain, and scouts reported that the hill was indeed undefended.

Ewell met with his division commanders, Jubal Early and Edward "Allegheny" Johnson, who commanded the elite "Stonewall Division" now approaching Gettysburg on the Chambersburg Pike. After a twenty-five-mile march the troops were delayed behind Hill's wagon train. It would take them at least an hour to reach the field, and there was now only two hours of daylight remaining. Johnson warned Ewell that his men may not reach the field in time.

Ewell reconsidered his options and ordered Johnson to take Culp's Hill with his division when they arrived but was only to advance if the hill remained unoccupied by the enemy—a **discretionary** order. Ewell then left for a con-

Major General Edward "Allegheny" Johnson

ference with Lee and the other corps commanders that did not end until almost midnight.

Johnson's men arrived after dark and were positioned around the base of Culp's Hill. With a discretionary order in hand, and perhaps unnerved by the prospect of advancing in darkness against an unknown enemy position (a rare event in Civil War battles), Johnston did not follow through on Ewell's orders to occupy the hill.

Thus, when Ewell returned to his command after midnight and discovered the situation, he ordered scouts to determine if Culp's Hill had been occupied by the enemy. Nearing the crest of the hill, lit by moonlight, the party was ambushed and fell back under heavy fire. Whatever chance there had been to seize Culp's Hill without a fight had passed, and a key opportunity to complete the day's victory lost.

> *Always mystify, mislead, and surprise the enemy, if possible; and when you strike and overcome him, never let up in the pursuit so long as your men have strength to follow; for an army routed, if hotly pursued, becomes panic-stricken, and can then be destroyed by half their number.*
>
> —Lieutenant General Thomas "Stonewall" Jackson

General Ewell had performed magnificently the entire campaign up to this point, marching his corps to Gettysburg in perfect timing to crush the Union Eleventh Corps that morning. Yet here, at a critical moment of the battle, he left the decision to advance on Culp's Hill to a subordinate and failed to oversee that his orders were carried out. The result of this indecisiveness would prove costly beyond measure. As Union reinforcements arrived throughout the night the Union line was fortified with trenches and **breastworks** of logs and stone. The Confederates were sure to face a formidable position by morning.

ELIZABETH SALOME "SALLIE" MYERS BECOMES A NURSE

Sallie Myers was called along with other women to assist the wounded. The Catholic church was just down the street from her father's home and she went to volunteer however she could. She had always feared the sight of blood and was terrified what might be asked of her.

On pews and floors men lay, the groans of the suffering and dying were heart-rending. I knelt beside the first man near the door and asked what I could do. "Nothing," he replied, "I am going to die." I went outside the church and cried. I returned and spoke to the

man—he was wounded in the lungs and spine, and there was not the slightest hope for him. The man was Sergeant Alexander Stewart of the 149th Pennsylvania Volunteers. I read a chapter of the Bible to him, it was the last chapter his father had read before he left home. The wounded man died on Monday, July 6th.

Sergeant Stewart was the first wounded man brought in, but others followed. The sight of blood never again affected me and I was among wounded and dying men day and night. While the battle lasted and the town was in possession of the rebels, I went back and forth between my home and the hospitals without fear. The soldiers called me brave, but I am afraid the truth was that I did not know enough to be afraid and if I had known enough, I had no time to think of the risk I ran, for my heart and hands were full.

THE 6TH WISCONSIN DIGS IN ON CULP'S HILL

Rufus Dawes recalled the early evening hours on Culp's Hill with his men. His 6th Wisconsin regiment had marched hard and fought all day, had suffered over 50 percent casualties, and yet had managed to make a fighting retreat in good order to their current position.

Then without even having anything to eat, the men began digging in, preparing for the upcoming fight they knew was close at hand. Dawes reflected:

Taking our place on the right of the line of the brigade, I ordered the regiment to entrench. The men worked with great energy . . . There were no orders to construct these breastworks, but the situation plainly dictated their necessity.

The men now lay down to rest after the arduous labors of this great and terrible day. Sad and solemn reflections possessed, at least, the writer of these papers. Our dead lay unburied and beyond our sight or reach. Our wounded were in the hands of the enemy. Our bravest and best were numbered with them. Of eighteen hundred men who marched with the splendid brigade in the morning, but seven hundred were here.

We had been driven, also, by the enemy, and the shadow of defeat seemed to be hanging over us. But that afternoon, under the burning sun and through the stifling clouds of dust, the Army of the Potomac has marched to the sound of our cannon. We had lost the ground on which we had fought, we had lost our commander and our comrades, but our fight had held the Cemetery Hill and forced the decision for history that the crowning battle of the war should be at Gettysburg.

FREMANTLE PREDICTS THE COMING STORM

Colonel Freemantle, accompanying Longstreet that evening, heard the opinions of the Confederate officers:

At supper this evening, General Longstreet spoke of the enemy's position as being "very formidable." He also said that they would doubtless entrench themselves strongly during the night. The Staff officers spoke of the battle as a certainty, and the universal feeling in the army was one of profound contempt for an enemy whom they have beaten so constantly, and under so many disadvantages . . . In the fight to-day nearly six-thousand prisoners had been taken, and ten guns. About twenty-thousand men must have been on the field on the Confederate side. The enemy had two corps engaged. All the prisoners belong to the First and Eleventh corps. This day's work is called a "brisk little scurry," and all anticipate a "big battle" tomorrow.

The Jacob Weikert barn as it appears today. Photo credit: The Gettysburg Daily.

DANIEL FINDS HIS HOME OCCUPIED BY REBELS

Daniel returned home that evening and found that his street had become part of the battlefield:

> *When I went out in front of the house about 7 o'clock in the evening, the Confederate line of battle had been formed on East and West Middle Streets, Rodes Division of Ewell's Corps lying right in front of our house. We were now in the hands of the enemy . . . these veterans of the Confederate Army were under perfect discipline. They were in and about our yard and used our kitchen stove by permission of my mother . . . gentlemanly and courteous to us at all times . . . We settled down quietly this night. There was no noise or confusion among the Confederate soldiers sleeping on the pavement below our windows and we all enjoyed a good night's rest after the feverish anxiety of the first day's battle.*

TILLIE BECOMES A NURSE FOR THE WOUNDED

Tillie Pierce remembered the final hours of July 1, as the wounded began arriving at the Weikert farm seeking aid and shelter:

It was toward the close of the afternoon of this day that some of the wounded from the field of battle began to arrive where I was staying. They reported hard fighting, many wounded and killed, and were afraid our troops would be defeated and perhaps routed.

The first wounded soldier whom I met had his thumb tied up. This I thought was dreadful, and told him so.

"Oh," said he, "this is nothing; you'll see worse than this before long."

"Oh! I hope not," I innocently replied.

Soon two officers carrying their arms in slings made their appearance, and I more fully began to realize that something terrible had taken place.

Now the wounded began to come in greater numbers. Some limping, some with their heads and arms in bandages, some crawling, others carried on stretchers or brought in ambulances. Suffering, cast down and dejected, it was a truly pitiable gathering. Before night the barn was filled with the shattered and dying heroes of this day's struggle.

That evening, Beckie Weikert, the daughter at home, and I went out to the barn to see what was transpiring there. Nothing before in my experience had ever paralleled the sight we then and there beheld. There were the groaning and crying, the struggling and dying, crowded side by side, while attendants sought to aid and relieve them as best they could.

We were so overcome by the sad and awful spectacle that we hastened back to the house weeping bitterly.

As we entered the basement or cellar-kitchen of the house, we found many nurses making beef tea for the wounded . . . a chaplain who was present in the kitchen stepped up to me while I was attending to some duty and said:

"Little girl, do all you can for the poor soldiers and the Lord will reward you."

The first day had passed, and with the rest of the family, I retired, surrounded with strange and appalling events, and many new visions passing rapidly through my mind.

THE MOONLIT NIGHT OF JULY 1

General Carl Schurz of the Union Eleventh Corps recalled the moonlit battlefield on the night of July 1: "We of the Eleventh Corps occupying the cemetery, lay down, wrapped in cloaks, with the troops among the grave stones. There was profound stillness in the graveyard, broken by no sound but the breathing of the men and here and there the tramp of a horse's foot; and sullen rumblings mysteriously floating on the air from a distance all around." Throughout the night both armies gathered and rested before dawn.

In the dim moonlight beyond the lines moved lanterns, like fireflies, as men searched for wounded comrades. By unspoken mutual consent, neither side would fire on those performing such missions of mercy. In the darkness, the cries of the wounded begging for help, for water, and some for their loved ones could be heard by the soldiers in the line. Each side did the best they could to retrieve the wounded who could be reached.

Among these men was Dr. LeGrand Wilson from Jackson, Mississippi. Searching through the thousands of wounded and dying men by lantern and under the full moon he later wrote of his efforts to save as many as he could: "This was my first experience on the battlefield after the fighting. And it was horrible beyond description. If every human being could have witnessed the result of the mad passions of men I saw that night, war would cease. There would never be another battle."

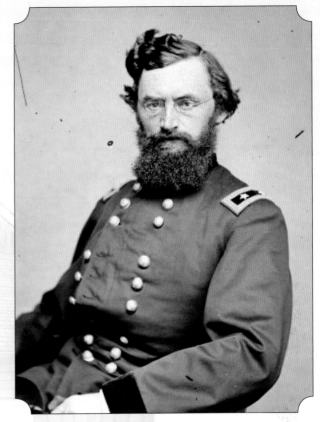

Major General Carl Schurz

Tillie Meets General Meade

Tillie awoke at the Weikert farmstead and knew it would be another blistering hot day:

The day dawned bright and clear; the hot rays of the July sun soon fell upon the landscape.

As quickly as possible I hurried out of the house, and saw more troops hurrying toward town.

About ten o'clock many pieces of artillery and large ammunition trains came up, filling the open space to the east of us.

Regiment after regiment continued to press forward. I soon engaged in the occupation of the previous day; that of carrying water to the soldiers as they passed . . . and while still supplying water to the passing troops, from the pump, three officers on horseback came riding up to the gate. The centre one kindly requested me to give him a drink. I asked him to please excuse the tin cup I then held in my hand. He replied:

"Certainly; that is all right."

After he had drunk he thanked me very pleasantly. The other two officers did not wish any.

As they were about turning away, the soldiers around gave three cheers for General Meade. The one to whom I had given the drink turned his horse about, made me a nice bow, and then saluted

the soldiers. They then rode rapidly away. I asked a soldier:

"Who did you say that officer was?"

He replied:

"General Meade."

Daniel Sees General Lee

Daniel woke that morning to find Gettysburg still occupied by Confederate soldiers. The rebels had thrown up barricades in the streets to defend against any Union attack.

Day dawned on the second of July bright and clear, and we did not know what to do or expect; whether to remain quietly in our homes, or go out in the town as usual and mingle with our people. But we were soon assured that if we kept within certain restrictions we could go about the town. It was hot and sultry and the lines of battle were quiet with the exception of an occasional exchange of shots between pickets or sharpshooters.

Some time during the morning in front of my home on West Middle Street . . . I was in conversation with one of the Confederate soldiers, whose regiment lay along the street in line of battle, when he asked me if I had ever seen General Lee. I replied that I had not. "Well," he said, "here he comes up the street on horseback." The general rode quietly by unattended and without any apparent recognition from the Confeder-

ate soldiers along the street. He reached Baltimore Street, about a square away at the court house, and turned into it going up to High Street.

LEE PLANS TO ATTACK MEADE'S LEFT FLANK

The peacefulness of the summer morning could not hide the fear of what the Union soldiers knew would come. Lee, having won the first day of battle, would certainly order an attack.

At the close of the first day, Lee met with Longstreet, who advised his commander not to attack the Union defenses. He told his commanding general, "If we could have chosen a point to meet our plans of operation, I do not think we could have found a better one than that upon which they are now concentrating. All we have to do is to throw our army around by their left, and we shall interpose between the Federal army and Washington . . . the Federals will be sure to attack us. When they

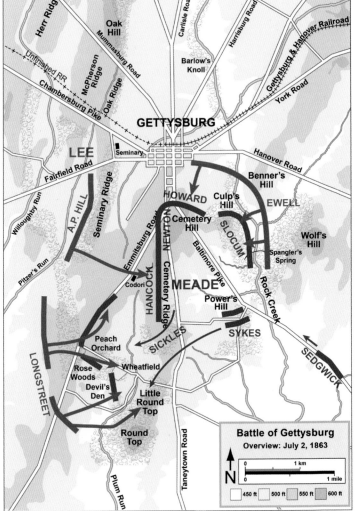

Map by Hal Jespersen, www.cwmaps.com.

attack, we shall beat them . . . and the probabilities are that the fruits of our success will be great."

Lee disagreed: "No, the enemy is there, and I am going to attack him there."

Longstreet knew that the Union position was strong and that any attack the following day could only succeed at a very great cost to the South. He pushed Lee to reconsider, but the general answered, "No; they are there in position, and I am going to whip them or they are going to whip me."

The night of July 1, Lee conferred with his corps commanders. Could they attack in the morning on the left against Culp's Hill? Ewell and Hill argued against it. Culp's Hill would be heavily fortified by morning. Their troops had marched and fought hard all day. Hill's troops, in particular, had suffered heavy casualties. Nor did the two generals advocate maneuvering away from Gettysburg to fight elsewhere—to order the men away from their hard won victory would be a devastating blow to the **morale** of Lee's army. And then there were the wounded to consider. With thousands of wounded men it would be impossible to withdraw and maneuver to a new position in the face of the enemy.

By morning it was clear to Lee that if he was to fight it would have to be with Longstreet's First Corps, with his two divisions under Generals John Bell Hood and

Lafayette McLaws. Lee planned to attack the Union left flank with a surprise assault up the Emmitsburg Road, supported by a third division under General Richard H. Anderson of Hill's corps to attack the Union center along Cemetery Ridge. Ewell's corps would make a **diversionary** assault against Culp's Hill to prevent those defenders from reinforcing the Union left. If the element of surprise could be achieved by Longstreet's corps, it could be as decisive a victory as Lee had won at Chancellorsville.

That morning, Longstreet still hoped to convince Lee to make a flanking movement and avoid a costly attack against the Union lines. Yet Lee would have none of it. A flanking movement would expose his army to attack. The Confederates had won the first day of the battle. If he attacked now he still had a chance to destroy part of the Army of the Potomac before all of its seven infantry corps could assemble. Longstreet was ordered to advance without waiting for Major General George Pickett's division, which was still marching toward Gettysburg.

General Hood arrived just after dawn that morning with his division's advance brigades. He saw Lee "with coat buttoned to the throat, saber-belt buckled round the waist, and field glasses pending at his side—walking up and down in the shade of the large trees near us, halting now and then to observe the enemy. He

Decision at Dawn—July 2, 1863. General Robert E. Lee surveys the Union position from a tree line along Seminary Ridge. While in quiet thought as to his next move, Lieutenant Colonel Charles Marshall, Major John W. Fairfax, and Lieutenant General A. P. Hill await his decision. Illustrated by Don Troiani.

seemed full of hope, yet, at time, buried in deep thought. Colonel Freemantle, of England, was ensconced in the forks of a tree not far off, with glass in constant use, examining the lofty position of the Federal Army."

Longstreet sat next to Hood against a tree and remarked, "The General is a little nervous this morning; he wishes me to attack; I do not wish to do so without Pickett. I never like to go into battle with one boot off."

Just after midday the troops began marching south toward their starting line across the Emmitsburg Road. The Confederates maneuvered behind Seminary Ridge to screen their movements from Union observers. It would take them several hours to reach their destination and deploy for battle. Longstreet would send the three divisions forward **en echelon** one after the other, like waves crashing along a beach, in an all-out attack to break the Union line.

GENERAL SICKLES MOVES THE THIRD CORPS

Just as the Confederates began moving into their attack positions, Meade's defensive plan began to unravel. A report arrived at Meade's headquarters that Sickles's Third Corps had not deployed to their positions along Cemetery Ridge as ordered, as Sickles was apparently confused. His troops had been ordered to defend

Major General Daniel Sickles. Photo credit: Library of Congress.

the southern third of Cemetery Ridge, linking in with Hancock's Fifth Corps to the right and anchoring the left on Little Round Top.

Sickles arrived at Meade's headquarters to complain that the position he was ordered to defend was poor ground for his men. Did he have the authority to adjust his lines to find ground better suited for artillery? Meade replied that he could, within the limits of his instructions. Sickles returned to his corps and hatched a plan that would surprise everyone, North and South, by the time he was done. At 2:00 PM, without informing Meade, Sickles ordered the Third Corps to advance 1,500 yards and to occupy a small ridgeline that ran along the Emmitsburg Road. His new extended line ran through a farmer's land, forever known afterward as the Peach Orchard and the Wheatfield.

Lieutenant Frank Haskell witnessed the advance of the Third Corps: "It was magnificent to see those ten or twelve thousand men—they were good men—with their batteries, and some squadrons of cavalry upon the left flank, all in battle order, in several lines, with flags streaming, sweep steadily down the slope, across the valley, and up the next ascent, toward their destined position! From our position we could see it all. In advance, Sickles pushed forward his heavy line of skirmishers, who drove back those of the enemy, across the Emmetsburg road [sic], and thus cleared the way for the main body.

The Third Corps now became the absorbing object of interest of all eyes."

By moving the 10,000 soldiers in his corps so far in advance of the main Union line, Sickles broke with the units to his right and formed a salient, or advance, position. The ground he chose, running through a peach orchard and wheat field, was open to attack on either flank. Meade rode out to confront Sickles, who then offered to pull his corps back into the line. Meade responded, "I wish to God you could, but the enemy won't let you." Within moments, the Confederate artillery opened fire on the exposed Third Corps, pinning it in place.

Major General John Bell Hood. Photo credit: The Photographic History of The Civil War in Ten Volumes.

LONGSTREET ORDERS THE ADVANCE ON THE UNION LEFT

The Third Corps' advance into the peach orchard also came as a surprise to the Confederates. As they arrayed for battle across the Emmitsburg Road around 3:00 PM, Longstreet discovered the Union lines had changed. Lee's plan had been to launch a flank attack against the Union's left. But Longstreet's two divisions now faced a heavily defended line of infantry and guns directly in their path. Worse still, the terrain over which this assault would be made was blocked by wood-and-stone fences, a meandering stream called Plum Run, and a valley of huge boulders and broken stone that locals called the Devil's Den. It would be impossible to keep the units together moving through such terrain under heavy enemy fire.

Hood knew what would happen if he sent his division forward under those conditions: "I knew that if the feat was accomplished, it must be at a most fearful sacrifice of as brave and **gallant** soldiers as ever engaged in battle."

"

I was introduced to General Hood this morning; he is a tall, thin, wiry-looking man, with a grave face and a light-colored beard, thirty-three years old, and is accounted one of the best and most promising officers in the army . . . His troops are accused of being a wild set, and difficult to manage; and it is the great object of the chiefs to check their innate plundering propensities by every means in their power.

"

—Colonel Arthur James Lyon Fremantle

Therefore, Hood sent his Texan scouts ahead to find a better line of attack. They quickly reported that east of Big Round Top there were no Union defenders at all. Even more **tantalizing**, the Federal army's wagon trains were sighted along the Taneytown Road. If Hood was allowed to shift his division to the right he could flank the Union army and attack from behind. He sent Longstreet repeated messages for permission to move his men to the east, but each time Longstreet replied, "General Lee's orders are to attack up the Emmitsburg road."

It was 4:30 PM and time was running short. Hood recalled the moment: "After this urgent protest against entering the battle at Gettysburg, according to instructions—which in protest is the first and only one I ever made during my entire military career—I ordered my line to advance and make the assault." Just as the order to advance was being given, Longstreet rode

up to Hood, who made a last attempt to gain permission to move his men to the east. Longstreet made it clear, "We must obey the orders of General Lee." Hood turned in his saddle and led his men into action: "Fix bayonets, my brave Texans! Forward and take those heights!" Twenty minutes later he was hit by a shell fragment to the left arm and carried from the field.

HOOD ATTACKS THE DEVIL'S DEN

When Meade learned that Sickles had advanced his corps into the Peach Orchard in advance of the Union line, he made two critical decisions: He ordered his only infantry reserve, Sykes's Fifth Corps, to advance into line in support of Sickles on the left; and he also ordered Gouverneur Warren up to Little Round Top to inspect its defenses after Sickles's unauthorized advance of his corps.

Just as the Fifth Corps began to arrive on the field Meade's army came under attack. Hood's division was advancing on Sickles's exposed Third Corps in the valley below Cemetery Ridge. As the armies met in battle, the ground at Devil's Den, the Wheatfield, and Peach Orchard soaked up the blood of Americans flowing into the soil. Lieutenant Haskell witnessed the assault from atop Cemetery Ridge:

Major General George Sykes.
Photo credit: Matthew Brady, Library of Congress.

First we hear more artillery firing upon Sickles' left—the enemy seems to be opening again, and as we watch the Rebel batteries seem to be advancing there . . . The position of the Third Corps becomes at once one of great peril . . .

All was astir now on our crest. Generals and their Staffs were galloping hither and thither—the men were all in their places, and you might have heard the rattle of ten thousand ramrods as they drove home and "thugged" upon the little globes and cones of lead.

Now came the dreadful battle picture . . . upon the front and right flank of Sickles came sweeping the infantry of Longstreet and Hill . . . the battle began; for amid the heavier smoke and larger tongues of flame of the batteries, now began to appear the countless flashes, and the long fiery sheets of the muskets, and the rattle of the volleys, mingled with the thunder of the guns. We see the long gray lines come sweeping down upon Sickles' front, and mix with the battle smoke; now the same colors emerge from the bushes and orchards upon his right, and envelope his flank in the confusion of the conflict.

O, the din and the roar, and these thirty thousand Rebel wolf cries! What a hell is there down that valley!

81

*Brigadier General
Strong Vincent*

advancing straight toward this spot. Warren immediately sent a message to Meade as staff officers raced in every direction seeking reinforcements to defend the heights. Warren knew that if the rebels were to seize control of Little Round Top, their artillery would be able to fire down on Cemetery Ridge and the battle would be lost for the Union.

Fifth Corps commander Sykes responded to Warren's call and ordered his First Division to occupy Little Round Top. His messenger was intercepted by Brigadier General Strong Vincent, commander of the Third Brigade, and hearing of the impending attack, Strong knew there was no time to lose. He took it upon himself to lead his own brigade up to Little Round Top to prevent its capture. He successfully deployed his four regiments only ten minutes before the Confederates arrived.

On the far left of Vincent's line was the 20th Maine Regiment under the command of Colonel Joshua Lawrence Chamberlain, a college-professor-turned-volunteer-soldier. Under

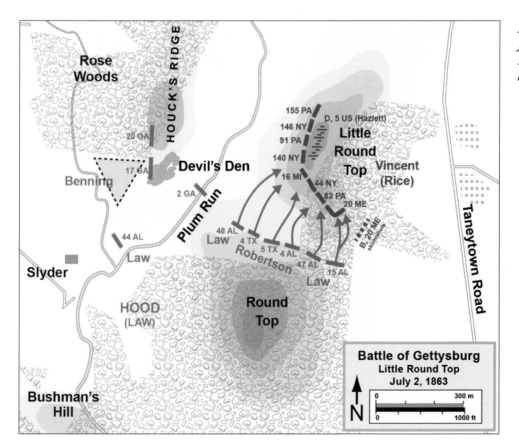

Map Little Round Top July 2 1863. Map by Hal Jespersen, www. cwmaps.com.

his command were 385 soldiers—veterans of the battle at Fredericksburg seven months earlier—who were all determined to make a stand. Chamberlain remembered the fateful hour:

Reaching the southern face of Little Round Top, I found Vincent there, with intense poise and look. He said with a voice of awe . . . "I place you here! This is the left of the Union line. You understand. You are to hold this ground at all costs!" I did understand—full well; but had more to learn about costs . . . This was the last word I heard from him.

The other regiments of the brigade were forming on our right; the Eighty-third Pennsylvania, the 54th New York, and the 16th Michigan . . . The enemy

Colonel Joshua Lawrence Chamberlain.
Photo credit: Matthew Brady, Library of Congress.

Colonel William Calvin Oates, 15th Alabama

had already turned the Third Corps left, the Devil's Den was a smoking crater, the Plum Run gorge was a whirling maelstrom; one force was charging our advanced batteries near the Wheat-field; the flanking force was pressing past the base of the Round Tops; all rolling towards us in tumultuous waves.

In a minute more came the roll of musketry. It struck the exposed right center of our brigade.

Promptly answered, repulsed, and renewed again and again, it

Little Round Top—July 2, 1863. On a hot July 2, 1863, the men of the 5th Texas advanced up the rocky slope to the climax of their ill-fated assault on Little Round Top. Illustrated by Don Troiani.

soon reached us, still extending. Two brigades of Hood's Division had at-tacked—Texas and Alabama. The 4th Alabama reached our right, the 47th Alabama joined and crowded in . . . Soon seven companies of this regiment were in our front. We had all we could stand.

To the right of the 47th Alabama was the 15th Alabama under Colonel William C. Oates. When the initial Federal volley halted the Confederate advance, Oates moved his regiment to the right, seeking to flank the Federal position. In doing so they came face-to-face with Chamberlain's 20th Maine. Oates recalled, "I ordered my regiment to drive the Federals from the ledge of rocks, gain the enemy's rear, and drive him from the hill. My men obeyed and advanced about half way to the enemy's position, but the fire was so destructive that my line wavered like a man trying to walk against a strong wind, and then slowly, doggedly, gave back a little."

Theodore Gerrish of the 20th Maine described the action:

> I wish that I could picture with my pen the awful details of that hour—how rapidly the cartridges were torn from the boxes and stuffed in the smoking muzzles of the guns; how the steel rammers clashed and clanged in the heated barrels; how the men's hands and faces grew grim and black with burning powder; how our little line, baptized with fire, reeled to and fro as it advanced or was pressed back; how our officers bravely encouraged the men to hold and recklessly exposed themselves to the enemy's fire—a terrible medley of cries, shouts, cheers, groans, prayers, curses, bursting shells, whizzing rifle bullets and clanging steel.

As the 15th Alabama moved further to the right to outflank the 20th Maine, Chamberlain realized the impending danger. Placing his colors at the center he ordered his officers to "refuse the line," moving half his men at a right angle to face the new threat. The Confederates charged, only to receive a deadly volley by this new wing of the 20th Maine at a range of ten paces. Chamberlain reported:

> From that moment began a struggle fierce and bloody beyond any that I have witnessed and which lasted in all its fury a full hour . . . The two lines met and broke and mingled in the shock. The crush of musketry gave way to cuts and thrusts, grapplings and wrestlings. The edge of conflict swayed to and from, with wild whirlpools and eddies. At times I saw around me more of the enemy than of my own men . . . All around, strange, mingled roar-shouts of defiance, rally, and desperation; and underneath, murmured entreaty and stifled moans; gasping prayers, snatches of Sabbath song, whispers of loved names; everywhere men torn and broken, staggering, creeping quivering on the earth, and dead faces with strangely fixed eyes staring stark into the sky.

The 20th Maine repulsed two more charges by the 15th Alabama. Forced back from their original defenses, though, their situation was now desperate. Their line had been pushed back, their ammunition was almost depleted, and many were wounded. Private Gerrish remembered: "A critical moment has arrived, and we can remain as we are no longer; we must advance or retreat." Chamberlain knew he had to act:

It was for us, then, once for all. Our thin line was broken, and the enemy were in rear of the whole Round Top defense . . . our fire was slackening; our last rounds of shot had been fired; what I had sent for could not get to us. I saw the faces of my men one after another, when they had fired their last cartridge, turn anxiously towards mine for a moment; then square to the front again. To the front for them lay death; to the rear what they would die to save.

Not a moment was to be lost! Desperate as the chances were, there was nothing for it, but to take the offensive. I stepped to the colors. The men turned towards me. One word was enough, "BAYONET!" It caught like fire and swept along the

Bayonet—July 2, 1863. Colonel Joshua L. Chamberlain and the men of the 20th Maine hold the far left of the Union line at the base of Gettysburg's Little Round Top. Illustrated by Don Troiani.

> *The enemy was pouring a terrible fire upon us, his superior forces giving him a great advantage. . . . The air seemed to be alive with lead. The lines at times were so near each other that the hostile gun barrels almost touched. . . . At one time there was a brief lull in the carnage, and our shattered line was closed up, but soon the contest raged again with renewed fierceness. . . . Many of our companies have suffered fearfully. . . . But there is no relief and the carnage goes on.*
>
> —Private Theodore Gerrish, 20th Maine

ranks. The men took it up with a shout . . . The grating clash of steel in fixing bayonets told its own story; the color rose in front; the whole line quivered for the start; the edge of the left-wing rippled, swung, tossed among the rocks, straightened, changed curve from scimitar to sickle-shape; and the bristling archers swooped down . . . into the face of half a thousand! Two hundred men!

The Federal charge took the Confederates by surprise. Oates was now in a compromised position. He ordered his men to retreat. Chamberlain's men captured hundreds of prisoners from both the 15th and 47th Alabama regiments. The price of this victory was steep— nearly half of the 20th Maine—185 men—were

killed, wounded, or missing. Oates reported nearly identical losses—161 casualties, including the death of Lieutenant John A. Oates, his younger brother.

Chamberlain's losses were not in vain, though. The left wing of Meade's army had been saved. Oates later wrote, "General Lee was never so close to victory as that day on Little Round Top . . . There was no better regiment in the Confederate Army than the 15th Alabama, and if it failed to carry any point against which it was thrown, no other single regiment need try it . . . There never were harder fighters than the 20th Maine and their gallant Colonel. His skill and persistence and the great bravery of his men saved Little Round Top, and the Army of the Potomac,

> *At the first dash the commanding officer I happened to confront, coming on fiercely, sword in one hand and big navy revolver in the other, fires one barrel almost in my face; but seeing the quick saber-point at his throat, reverses arms, gives sword and pistol into my hands and yields himself prisoner.*
>
> —Colonel Joshua Lawrence Chamberlain, 20th Maine

from defeat. Great events sometimes turn on comparatively small affairs."

Among the fallen on Little Round Top was Brigadier General Stephen H. Weed, commander of a brigade sent to reinforce Vincent's command in the opening moments of the fighting. Mortally wounded by an enemy sharpshooter he was carried to the Weikert farm, where he would receive aid from a young school girl—Tillie Pierce.

HOOD AND MCLAWS ATTACK THE WHEAT FIELD

At the center of the Third Corps' line was a twenty-acre wheat field owned by famer John Rose. Colonel Régis de Trobriand commanded a brigade in Sickles's Third Corps assigned to defend this key piece of terrain. It was here alongside the Peach Orchard and the Rose Woods to the west that the Confederates struck, attempting to force their way past the Third Corps and onto Cemetery Ridge, which lay beyond. Trobriand remembered the attack:

A burst of cheering, followed immediately by a violent musketry fire, told us that the rebels were charging across the ravine . . . I had then but two regiments in line of battle, and a third prolonging my line as skirmishers, when the avalanche rolled upon me. Hold on there, hard and firm! There is no reserve!

It was a hard fight. The Confederates appeared to have the devil in them . . . On the other side, my men did not flinch . . . Like veterans, accustomed to make the best of every resource, they sheltered themselves behind the rocks and trunks of trees which were on the line, and when their assailants descended into the ravine and crossed the creek they were received, at a distance of twenty yards, with a deadly volley, every shot of which was effective.

The assault broken, those who were on the opposite slope began a rapid fire at a range still very short. On both sides, each one aimed at his man, and, notwithstanding every protection from the ground, men fell dead and wounded with frightful rapidity. The persistent pressure of the attack showed clearly that we had a contest with superior forces. If they had attacked us entirely with bayonet, we would have been swept away.

So we maintained our hold; but my line was melting away in its position. It seemed to me that nearly half were struck down . . . Our position was no longer tenable; our ammunition was nearly exhausted, and already some of the men were searching the cartridge boxes of the dead for ammunition, when, at last, a brigade of the Second Corps came to relieve us . . .

The enemy, profiting by our movement in retreat, had advanced into the wheat field, on the edge of which I rallied what remained to me of the 5th Michigan and 110th Pennsylvania. General Birney, who was near, immediately brought into line of battle the 17th Maine and a New Jersey regiment of Burling's brigade. I hastened to complete the line with troops I had at hand, and we charged through the wheat field, driving the rebels back to the other side of the stone wall. It was the first charge of the day on that ground which saw so many more before night. It was also the last effort of my brigade.

GENERAL BARKSDALE'S CHARGE

Among McLaws's brigades attacking Sickles's line was Brigadier General William Barksdale's Mississippians. Originally from Tennessee, Barksdale was from one of the wealthiest families of the South and a **firebrand** pro-slavery politician. A combat veteran of the Mexican War he held a passionate hatred for the Yankees.

At 5:30 PM, his brigade was in position with McLaw's division to assault eastward, across the Emmitsburg Road and into Sickles's line in the Peach Orchard, then onward toward Little Round Top and Cemetery Ridge. Impatient to attack, Barksdale knew his time for glory had come.

Barksdale's Charge—July 2, 1863. General William Barksdale's brigade, the 17th Mississippi, descended on the Union position in the Peach Orchard bordering Gettysburg's Emmitsburg Road. Illustrated by Don Troiani.

Captain G. B. Lamar delivered the orders to advance and remembered, "Barksdale was radiant with joy. He was in front of his men with his hat off, and his long, white hair reminded me of the white plume of **Navarre**."

Private T. M. Scanlon of the 17th Mississippi recalled Barksdale's speech to his men prior to the charge:

Halt! Front! Order Arms! Load! Fix Bayonets!

The entrenchment 500 yards in front of you at the red barn, and that park of artillery as well as the cone mountain (Little Round Top) . . . we are also expected to take.

This is an heroic undertaking and most of us will bite the dust making this effort. Now if there is a man here that feels this is too much for him, just step two paces to the front and I will excuse him. We will proceed to within 75 yards of the entrenchment withholding our fire. There you will receive the command, Halt! Ready! Fire!, after which, without command you will charge with the bayonet.

Attention, Mississippians! Battalions forward! Dress to the colors and Forward to the foe! Onward, Brave Mississippians, for Glory!

Brigadier General William Barksdale

Leading his brigade on horseback, Barksdale's troops shattered the Union brigade opposing them in the Peach Orchard and advanced a mile into the Union line—as far as Plum Run near the base of Little Round Top and Cemetery Ridge. Hit three times, including a mortal chest wound, Barksdale was felled from his horse and yelled to an aide, "I am killed! Tell my wife and children that I died fighting at my post."

Barskdale's attack had penetrated the Union lines but was countered by reinforcements sent by Hancock to stop Longstreet's mighty assault. Overwhelmed by the Union's superior position, firepower, and sheer numbers, the Confederate attack was repulsed. Barksdale was captured and died that evening at a Union field hospital.

FATHER CORBY AND THE IRISH BRIGADE

As the Third Corps fought for its life against the Confederate attack, Hancock organized reinforcements to save the Union line. One of those units was the elite Irish Brigade under Colonel Patrick Kelly. The five veteran regiments of this brigade from New York and Massachusetts consisted of almost all Irish immigrants. Among them was Father William Corby, a Catholic priest. As the brigade formed near the wheat field and prepared to advance into the cauldron of battle that lay ahead, Corby recalled, "At this critical moment, I proposed to give a general **absolution** to our men, as they had absolutely no chance to practice their religious duties during the past two or three weeks, being constantly on the march."

Absolution Under Fire by Paul Wood, c. 1891. Print credit: Snite Museum of Art, University of Notre Dame.

> *In performing this ceremony I faced the army. My eye covered thousands of officers and men. I noticed that all, Catholic and non-Catholic, officers and private soldiers showed a profound respect, wishing at this fatal crisis to receive every benefit of divine grace that could be imparted through the instrumentality of the Church ministry. Even Major General Hancock removed his hat, and, as far as compatible with the situation, bowed in reverential devotion. That general absolution was intended for all—in quantum possum—not only for our brigade, but for all, North or South, who were susceptible of it and who were about to appear before their Judge.*

—Father William Corby

A fellow officer of the brigade, Colonel St. Clair Mulholland, wrote of the event as "the most impressive religious ceremonies I have ever witnessed":

Father Corby stood on a large rock in front of the brigade. Addressing the men, he explained what he was about to do, saying that each one could receive the benefit of the absolution by making a sincere Act of Contrition and firmly resolving to embrace the first opportunity of confessing his sins, urging them to do their duty, and reminding them of the high and sacred nature of their trust as soldiers and the noble object for which they fought.... The brigade was standing at "Order arms!" As he closed his address, every man, Catholic and non-Catholic, fell on his knees with his head bowed down. Then, stretching his right hand toward the brigade, Father Corby pronounced the words of the absolution:

"Dominus noster Jesus Christus vos absolvat..." May our Lord Jesus Christ absolve you; and I by his authority

The scene was more than impressive; it was awe inspiring. Nearby stood a brilliant throng of officers who had gathered to witness this very unusual occurrence, and while there was a profound silence in the ranks of the Second Corps, yet over to the left, out by the peach orchard and Little Round Top . . . the roar of the battle rose and swelled and re-echoed through the woods, making music more sublime than ever sounded through cathedral isle. The act seemed to be in harmony with the surroundings.

—Colonel St. Clair Mulholland

absolve you from every bond of excommunication and interdict, as far as I am able, and you have need. Moreover, I absolve you of your sins, in the name of the Father, and of the Son, and of the Holy Ghost. Amen."

The Irish Brigade, with the rest of the 1st Division, advanced into the wheat field moments later and stopped the Confederate attack by nightfall. Of the 530 men of the Irish Brigade, 200 were killed, wounded, or missing by the day's end.

Major General Richard Heron Anderson

ANDERSON ASSAULTS CEMETERY RIDGE

At 6:00 PM, Longstreet ordered Anderson's division of Hill's corps forward, the last of his en echelon attacks now attempting to storm Cemetery Ridge. The five-brigade attack was the final blow that routed Sickles's devastated Third Corps. Amid the desperate fighting around the Trostle farm, a canon shot nearly tore off Sickles's right leg. He was car-

Major General Lafayette McLaws

Brigadier General Cadmus Marcellus Wilcox

Colonel William J. Colvill

ried from the field, a cigar clenched between his teeth as a show of defiance for the men. When Meade learned of the news, he placed Hancock in command of both the Second and Third corps.

The fate of Sickles's Third Corps was already sealed. Assaulted from three sides by superior forces, the survivors of his two divisions were falling back toward Cemetery Ridge. Meade had moved all of his reserve infantry to reinforce the left of his line against Longstreet's flanking attack by Hood's and McLaws's divisions. The line at the center was thinly manned by just a few batteries of cannons and almost no supporting infantry. It was at this weakly defended point that Anderson's attack was aimed.

Riding to the crest of Cemetery Ridge, Hancock witnessed the lead enemy brigade advancing straight for a gap in the Union line. Hancock knew he had no choice but to order his only infantry reserve forward. This was the 262-man 1st Minnesota Regiment under Colonel William Colvill. Advancing on them

First Minnesota—July 2, 1863. Overlooking the battlefield at Gettysburg, the 1st Minnesota Volunteer Infantry could see their lines crumbling under Confederate attack. At that moment, Union Second Corps Commander Winfield Scott Hancock galloped up and in desperation ordered the Minnesotans forward. Illustrated by Don Troiani.

was an entire Confederate brigade—almost 1,800 men—under Brigadier General Cadmus Wilcox.

Pointing at the Confederate flag of Wilcox's brigade, Hancock yelled to Colvill, "Advance, Colonel, and take those colors!" Lieutenant William Lochren remembered, "Every man realized in an instant what that order meant; death or wounds to us all, the sacrifice of the regiment, to gain a few minutes' time and save the position and probably the battle-field." Without hesitation, the 1st Minnesota, knowing what was being asked of them, fixed bayonets and charged toward the Confederate soldiers. Their courageous attack caught the enemy by surprise, halted their advance, and force them to unleash a deadly volley into the charging Union troops.

July 2nd 1863

Should any person find this on the body of a soldier on the field of battle or by the roadside they will confer a lasting favor on the parents of its owner by sending the book & pocket perce & silver finger ring on the left hand. Taking their pay for trouble out of the Greenbacks herein inclosed

Mat

To Seth Marvin Esq

St. Charles
Kane Co
Ill

Author's Note: Notation made on the inside cover of Private Matthew Marvin's leather bound diary, K Company, 1st Minnesota Regiment. Source: Minnesota Historical Society.

When Hancock ordered the 1st Minnesota forward, he thought their attack would buy him five minutes of time in which to reinforce the Union line. Fifteen minutes later, 215 men of the Minnesota regiment were killed, wounded, or missing, including Colvill, but the gallant few remaining held their ground. The 1st Minnesota has the distinction of sustaining the highest regimental losses in any battle, in proportion to the number engaged, in the Civil War.

Wilcox found his brigade under fire from three sides as Federal canon took aim at his men. Now facing Union reinforcements along Cemetery Ridge and unsupported by other brigades, Wilcox had no choice but to order his men to fall back. With this, the Union line had been saved. Hancock later wrote of this event, "I would have ordered that regiment in if I had known every man would have been killed, it had to be done . . . There is no more gallant deed recorded in history."

The repulse of Wilcox's brigade had a critical effect on the other attacking brigades adjacent to his. Brigadier General A. R. Wright's brigade advanced boldly toward Cemetery Ridge, smashing past line after line of defending Union soldiers. He relates:

We were now within less than 100 yards of the crest of the heights, which were lined by artillery, supported by a strong body of infantry, under protection of a stone fence. My men, by a well-directed fire, soon drove the cannoneers from their guns, and, leaping over the fence, charged up to the top of the crest, and drove the enemy's infantry . . . some 80 or 100 yards in the rear of the enemy's batteries. We were now complete masters of the field, having gained the key, as it were, of the enemy's whole line. Unfortunately, just as we had carried the enemy's last and strongest position it was discovered that the brigade on our right had not only not advanced across the turnpike, but had actually given way and was rapidly falling back to the rear, while on our left we were entirely unprotected, the brigade ordered to our support having failed to advance.

It was now evident, with my ranks so seriously thinned as they had been by this terrible charge, I should not be able to hold my position unless speedily and strongly reinforced . . . We were now in a critical condition. The enemy's converging line was rapidly closing upon our rear. A few moments more and we would be completely surrounded. Still no support could be seen coming to our assistance, and with painful hearts we abandoned our captured guns, faced about, and prepared to cut our way through the closing lines in our rear. In this charge my loss was very severe, amounting to 688 in killed, wounded, and missing, including many valuable officers.

Major General Henry Warner Slocum

Ewell Attacks Culp's Hill

As Longstreet attacked the Union army's left and center with three divisions, Meade was unaware that a final attack was about to fall on his right. Ewell prepared to send an entire division against Culp's Hill. If the heights were captured, Lee could then turn the Union flank and force the Army of the Potomac to withdraw or face destruction.

The attack opened with an artillery duel against Union batteries on Culp's Hill at 4:00 PM. Meade, desperate for reinforcements on the left against Longstreet's attacks, called on the Twelfth Corps occupying Culp's Hill. Believing that the artillery fire was only a demonstration, Meade ordered Major General Henry Slocum to send his entire corps to reinforce the Union left.

Slocum saw the danger ahead of him and requested to keep a division on Culp's Hill to protect the key position. Meade refused, but allowed him to keep a single brigade. Slocum chose the 3rd Brigade of the Twelfth Corp's

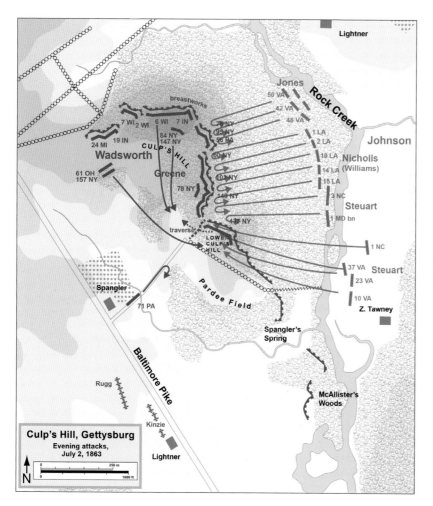

Brigadier General George Sears Greene

Map by Hal Jespersen, www.cwmaps.com.

Second Division, a veteran unit of New Yorkers led by sixty-two-year-old Brigadier General George Sears Greene of Rhode Island. A skilled combat engineer, Greene knew how to make the most of the terrain to strengthen his defenses. Working all day, his men had built an impressive trench and breastworks line near the crest of the hill with logs and stones. Now spread out along the trench line, his single brigade awaited the Confederate attack.

As dusk fell around 7:15 PM, skirmishers saw Confederate troops crossing Rock Creek at the base of the hill. In mere moments, Johnson's three brigades of rebel infantry advanced on Greene's breastworks. Major. W. Goldsborough of the 2nd Maryland Infantry described the advance: "The ground over which Johnson's Division moved was rough enough at first, but became much rougher after it had crossed Rock Creek and struck the wooded hill . . . Here immense rocks and boulders were encountered, which greatly retarded the progress of the troops, and darkness came on, and no enemy save a few skirmishers had been encountered."

Rufus Dawes and his 6th Wisconsin were deployed in Greene's line. Dawes later wrote, "A sound came now from the woods to our right that made us jump for our breastworks. It was the rebel yell, sounded by thousands of voices. It was almost dusk, and beginning to be quite dark in the woods. I ran to my post, and ordered: 'Down, men, watch sharp, keep your eyes peeled! Shoot low, shoot low, the hill is steep; quiet now; steady!'"

As the rebels advanced up the hill, Greene's men were ordered to fire. "Out into the night like chain-lightning leaped the zig-zag line of fire," recalled the 60th New York's Captain Jones. All along the line fighting raged for almost three hours. Johnson's men seized the abandoned fortifications at the base of Culp's Hill but advanced no further. As complete darkness fell around 10:00 PM, other Twelfth Corps brigades returned to their positions and were ordered to attack at first light. The ground was littered with the dead and wounded of both sides.

TILLIE HELPS THE WOUNDED

The fighting on Little Round Top had occurred perilously close to Jacob Weik-ert's farm where Tillie labored to help the wounded:

On this evening the number of wounded brought to the place was indeed appalling. They were laid in different parts of the house. The orchard and space around the buildings were covered with the shattered and dying, and the barn became more and more crowded. The scene had become terrible beyond description.

That night, in the house, I made myself useful in doing whatever I could to assist the surgeons and nurses. Cooking and making beef tea seemed to be going on all the time. It was an animated and busy scene. Some were cutting bread and spreading it, while I was kept busy carrying the pieces to the soldiers.

One soldier, sitting near the doorway that led into a little room in the southeast corner of the basement, beckoned me to him. He was holding a lighted candle in his hand, and was watching over a wounded soldier who was lying upon the floor. He asked me if I would get him a piece of bread, saying he was very hungry. I said certainly, ran away and soon returned. I gave him the bread and he seemed very thankful. He then asked me if I would hold the light and stay with the wounded man until he came back. I said I would gladly do so, and that I wanted to do something for the poor soldiers if I only knew what.

I then took the candle and sat down beside the wounded man. I talked to him and asked if he was injured badly. He answered:

"Yes, pretty badly."

I then asked him if he suffered much, to which he replied:

"Yes, I do now, but I hope in the morning I will be better."

I told him if there was anything I could do for him I would be so glad to do it, if he would only tell me what. The poor man looked so earnestly into my face, saying:

"Will you promise me to come back in the morning to see me."

I replied: "Yes, indeed." And he seemed so satisfied, and faintly smiled.

The man who had been watching him now returned, and thanked me for my kindness. I gave him the light and arose to leave.

The poor wounded soldier's eyes followed me, and the last words he said to me were:

"Now don't forget your promise." I replied:

"No indeed," and expressing the hope that he would be better in the morning, bade him good night.

DANIEL ATTEMPTS TO SPY FOR THE UNION

Overcome by excitement, Daniel met up with some of his friends that evening and tried to learn news of the battle by spying on Confederate soldiers:

The night of the second I slept in a room above the Fahnestock store with a number of other boys. Not making any light we would remain quietly at the window trying to catch the conversation of the Confederate soldiers who were lying on the pavement below the window. We were eager to catch something that would give us some clue to our army and how they were fairing in the battle . . . but did not learn much from them. We finally went to bed and settled down into a sound sleep as boys do who have few cares and sound health.

LEE PLANS TO CONTINUE THE ATTACK

As the guns fell silent with nightfall, each army withdrew to their lines and waited for dawn. Longstreet later declared that the assaults by his two divisions that day had been "the best three hour's fighting ever done by any troops on any battlefield." Yet he knew the attacks had ultimately failed to carry in their primary objective. The Union line remained intact along Cemetery Ridge, and Meade retained the high ground on either end of the battlefield. After sending a messenger to report to Lee on the placement and condition of his corps, Longstreet retired to his headquarters. Hoping to dissuade Lee from renewing the attack, Longstreet ordered scouts to the right of Culp's Hill, seeking a route to outmaneuver the Federal army the following day.

Around 10:00 PM orders arrived from Lee—the attack would continue the next day with Pickett's division against the Union center. Ewell was ordered to attack the Union right

Gettysburg Council of War by James E. Kelly. Image credit: U.S. Army Military History Institute.

sylvania to smash the Army of the Potomac and win the war. With Pickett's fresh division in the assault and Stuart's cavalry let loose on the enemy's rear, Lee was confident the Union could be forced off Cemetery Ridge and that the battle would be won.

MEADE PLANS TO FIGHT IT OUT

Meade held a conference of his corps commanders at the small one-room farmhouse on Cemetery Ridge that night. He had already telegraphed General Halleck in Washington, DC, that he intended to keep his army at Gettysburg. Yet Meade wished to hear the opinions of his generals if they agreed with this plan. In the small candlelit room a vote was taken. The generals made a unanimous agreement—the army would remain as it was currently deployed and await Lee's attack, if it came. They would only attack if Lee moved to cut off their communications and supply— which was exactly what Longstreet hoped to do.

Meade commented to General John Gibbon, acting commander of the Second Corps deployed on Cemetery Ridge, "If Lee attacks tomorrow, it will be in your front . . . he has made attacks on both our flanks and failed and if he concludes to try it again, it will be on our center." Meade knew that Lee still had Pickett's division, which had yet to be sent

Major General John Gibbon.
Photo credit: Library of Congress.

at first light, coordinating with Longstreet's assault. Stuart was ordered to take his cavalry division around the Union's right side on Culp's Hill and attack from behind. Artillery Chief William Pendleton was ordered to prepare a heavy **bombardment** of the Union positions along Cemetery Ridge. Lee had come to Penn-

into battle. If Lee attacked the following day, it would be with Pickett's men. Meade still held the high ground and almost all his artillery remained intact and in good supply. The Army of the Potomac had taken a savage beating, but they were prepared to fight another day.

Chapter Five

Friday, July 3, 1863

Gettysburg was the price the South paid for having Robert E. Lee as commander.

—Shelby Foote

TILLIE KEEPS HER PROMISE

Tillie was so tired from her work the night before that she didn't wake up until late in the morning:

The first thought that came into my mind, was my promise of the night before.

I hastened down to the little basement room, and as I entered, the soldier lay there—dead. His faithful attendant was still at his side.

I had kept my promise, but he was not there to greet me. I hope he greeted nearer and dearer faces than that of the unknown little girl on the battle-field of Gettysburg.

As I stood there gazing in sadness at the prostrate form, the attendant looked up to me and asked: "Do you know who this is?" I replied: "No sir." He said: "This is the body of General Weed; a New York man."

Brigadier General Stephen Hinsdale Weed

107

Mary Virginia Wade

morning of July 1, as the battle neared town, the Wades fled to the nearby home of Ginnie's sister, Georgia McClellan, and her newborn son on Baltimore Street. Ginnie spent most of the day distributing bread to Union soldiers and filling their canteens with water. She was determined to do everything she could for the men.

After the Union Army had retreated to Cemetery Hill, her sister's house lay between the armies. Confederate sharpshooters were firing at targets near the house, sometimes killing or wounding men in the yard or the nearby vacant lot. The cries of these wounded men made sleep impossible that night, and Ginnie risked her life to take water to these fallen soldiers. The women spent the next day handing out bread and water to any Union men who came knocking asking for food.

Early on the morning of July 3, Ginnie awoke early to bake more bread for the men. The day before, she and her mother had made yeast that they left in the kitchen to rise overnight. As Ginnie went about kneading the dough, the house came under fire from Confederate sharpshooters. Seeing movement in the house that the Confederates may have assumed to be Union soldiers taking cover in the kitchen, they opened fire. A bullet penetrated the outer door of the north side of the house, and a second door between the parlor and the kitchen, and hit Ginnie in the back under her shoulder blade. The bullet pierced her heart and killed her instantly.

Hearing the cries of Ginnie's mother and sister, Union soldiers came and helped wrap the young woman's body in a blanket and carried her to the basement. Ginnie's mother, assisted by the soldiers, later returned to the kitchen—now stained by her daughter's blood. Together they finished baking fifteen loaves of bread, all of which were given to the hungry men.

Ginnie Wade was the only civilian killed during the fighting at Gettysburg, and was hailed in the weeks to come as a national hero. Her name was misreported in the newspapers as Jennie Wade, and that is how history came to remember her.

THE BOMBARDMENT

Lieutenant Haskell saw Meade ride along Cemetery Ridge the morning of July 3, commenting that the general "rode along the whole line, looking to it himself, and with glass in hand sweeping the woods and fields in the direction of the enemy . . . . He was well pleased with the left of the line today, it was so strong with good troops. He had no apprehension for the right

Colonel Edward Porter Alexander.
Photo credit: The Photographic History
of The Civil War in Ten Volumes.

where the fight now was going on." If Lee did try to assault his center, Meade had two of his veteran divisions of Hancock's Second Corps defending Cemetery Ridge.

As the fighting on Culp's Hill ceased a strange quiet fell over the battlefield. The heat of the day lulled many to sleep, exhausted at their posts. Haskell recounted, "Eleven o'clock came. The noise of battle has ceased upon the right; not a sound of a gun or musket can be heard on all the field; the sky is bright, with only the white fleecy clouds floating over from the West. The July sun streams down its fire upon the bright iron of the muskets in stacks upon the crest, and the dazzling brass of the **Napoleons**. The army lolls and longs for the shade, of which some get a hand's breadth, from a shelter tent stuck upon a ramrod. The silence and sultriness of a July noon are supreme."

Yet across the way on Seminary Ridge, Colonel Edward Porter Alexander, Longstreet's corps artillery chief, was deploying over 163 cannons in a line over two miles long to bombard the Union center. Lee planned to make a concentrated strike against the Federal batteries along Cemetery Ridge to clear the way for a massive infantry assault of three divisions commanded by Trimble, Pettigrew, and Pickett. The nine infantry brigades would have to advance over a mile of open farmland and cross the Emmitsburg Road to assault the Union line. Pickett, a favorite of Longstreet's, would command the attack, and thus the ensuing battle would be forever remembered as Pickett's Charge.

War correspondent Charles Coffin was at Meade's headquarters when the firing began and later recalled:

Every size and form of shell known to British and to American gunnery shrieked, whirled, moaned, and whistled, and wrathfully fluttered over our ground. As many as six in a second, constantly two in a second, bursting and screaming over and around the head-quarters, made a very hell of fire that amazed the oldest officers. They burst in the yard,—burst next to the fence on both sides, garnished as usual with the hitched horses of aides and orderlies. The fastened animals reared and plunged with terror . . . sixteen lay dead and mangled before the fire ceased . . .

A shell tore up the little step at the head-quarters cottage, and ripped bags of oats as with a knife. Another soon carried off one of its two pillars. Soon a spherical case burst opposite the open door,—another ripped through the low garret. The remaining pillar went almost immediately to the howl of a fixed shot . . .

Forty minutes,—fifty minutes,—counted watches that ran, O so languidly! Shells through the two lower rooms. A shell into the chimney, that daringly did not explode. Shells in the yard. The air thicker, and fuller, and more deafening with the howling and whirring of these infernal missiles . . .

A shell exploding in the cemetery, killed and wounded twenty-seven men in one regiment! And yet the troops, lying under the fences,—stimulated and encouraged by General Howard, who walked coolly along the line,—kept their places and awaited the attack.

Amid this chaos, Hancock calmly rode his horse behind the ranks of his infantry taking cover along the wall. His calm, determined fearlessness was an inspiration to his men. When a subordinate officer complained of the risks he was taking Hancock replied, "There are times when the life of a corps commander does not count."

THE CAVALRY BATTLE: J. E. B. STUART VS. GEORGE CUSTER

As Pickett's Charge was about to move forward, Stuart led his entire cavalry division south from the York Pike toward the rear of the Union army. Stuart's cavalry would then circle behind the Union lines and cause **havoc** by attacking from behind. If Stuart could capture and hold the Baltimore Pike behind Culp's Hill, it would sever the enemy's communications and supply. Combined with Pickett's assault this attack posed a mortal threat to the Union army if properly executed.

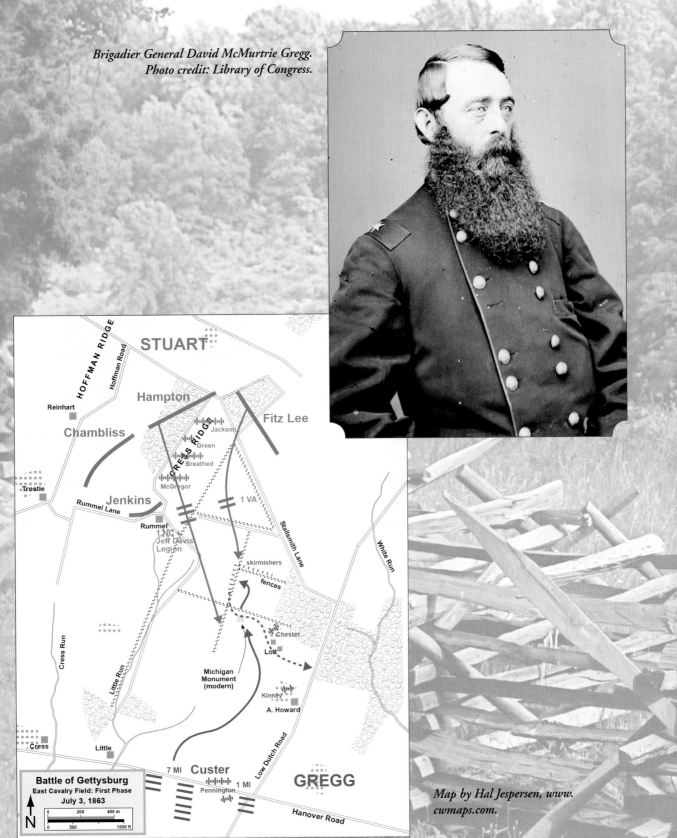

Brigadier General David McMurtrie Gregg.
Photo credit: Library of Congress.

Map by Hal Jespersen, www.
cwmaps.com.

117

*Brigadier General George Armstrong Custer.
Photo credit: George L. Andrews, National Archives.*

Directly in Stuart's path, however, were two brigades of union cavalry under Brigadier General David M. Gregg. One was commanded by Colonel John B. McIntosh and the other was a newly formed 7th Cavalry from Michigan under a firebrand officer Brigadier General George Armstrong Custer.

As the 1st Virginia Cavalry charged across a field to attack Union skirmishers, Gregg ordered Custer to lead a counter at-

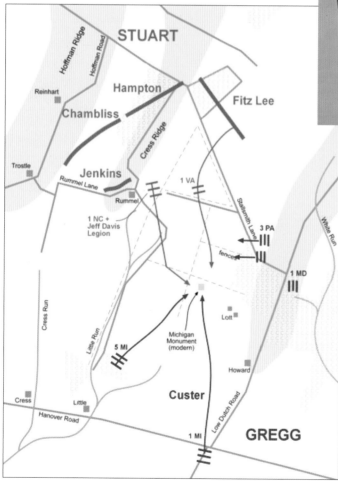

tack. Custer led his regiment forward crying, "Come on, you Wolverines!"

The ensuing combat between mounted cavalrymen was at point-blank range using sabers and pistols. Custer had his horse shot out from under him and without missing a beat, he took the mount of his bugler. The Virginians were forced back, only to have Stuart counterattack with troopers from all three of his brigades.

*Gettysburg East Cavalry Field, final actions.
Map by Hal Jespersen, www.cwmaps.com.*

Come on, you Wolverines! Custer leads the Michigan Brigade, Gettysburg—July 3, 1863. Illustrated by Don Troiani.

Again, Custer led the charge to meet the rebel horsemen midfield. A trooper remembered, "As the two columns approached each other the pace of each increased, when suddenly a crash, like the falling of timber, betokened the crisis. So sudden and violent was the collision that many of the horses were turned end over end and crushed their riders beneath them."

Attacked on three sides the Confederate forces were forced to pull back. Custer's brigade had lost over 200 men, and Stuart's command almost as many. But the fight was over. Stuart's cavalry had been stopped, and the threat to the Union rear was squelched. Pickett's infantry, about to make their assault on Cemetery Ridge a few miles away, would have to win the day on their own.

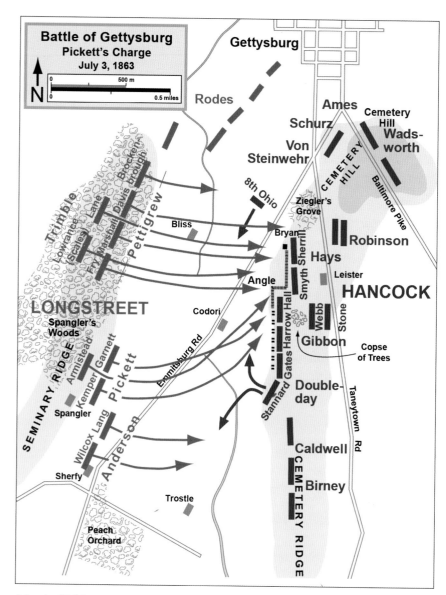

Battle of Gettysburg
Pickett's Charge
July 3, 1863

N

0   500 m
0   0.5 miles

Gettysburg

Rodes

Ames
Schurz
Von
Steinwehr
8th Ohio

Cemetery
Hill
Wads-
worth

CEMETERY HILL

Baltimore Pike

Brockenbrough
Davis
Marshall
Fry
Lowrance (Scales)
Lane
Trimble
Pettigrew

Bliss

Ziegler's
Grove

Bryan

Robinson

Smyth Sherrill

Angle

Hays

Leister

HANCOCK

LONGSTREET

Spangler's
Woods

SEMINARY RIDGE

Codori

Emmitsburg Rd

Stannard Gates Harrow Hall

Webb
Stone

Gibbon

Copse
of Trees

Armistead
Garnett
Kemper
Pickett

Spangler

Double-
day

Taneytown Rd

Wilcox Lang
Anderson

Sherfy

Caldwell

Birney

Trostle

CEMETERY RIDGE

Peach
Orchard

Map by Hal Jespersen, www.cwmaps.com.

The Confederate brigades planned to advance by marching almost a mile across the open fields, not stopping to fire until they reached the Emmitsburg Road, which lay two hundred yards from the Union line. All units would **converge** at the center of the Union line where a small copse of trees stood at a corner of the stone wall, forever known afterward as "the Angle." If the artillery had silenced the Union guns the infantry could then advance and attack Cemetery Ridge to split the Union line in two. Hill's corps was held in reserve to reinforce any breakthrough. Success or failure now rested entirely on the infantry.

"Regiment after regiment and brigade after brigade move from the woods and rapidly take their places in the lines forming the assault," reported Haskell. "More than half a mile their front extends; more than a thousand yards the dull gray masses deploy, man touching man, rank pressing rank, and line supporting line. The red flags wave, their horsemen gallop up and down; the arms of eighteen thousand men, barrel and bayonet, gleam in the sun, a sloping

Rock of Erin, July 3, 1863. The 69th Pennsylvania volunteer infantry defends Cemetery Ridge from Pickett's Charge. Illustrated by Don Troiani.

forest of flashing steel. Right on they move, as with one soul, in perfect order, without impediment of ditch, or wall or stream, over ridge and slope, through orchard and meadow, and cornfield, magnificent, grim, irresistible."

Waiting for the Confederates along the Union line were massed infantry four-ranks deep in some places, laying flat behind the wall with loaded muskets, ready for the time when the enemy would be within range. Charles Coffin witnessed the advance: "Every man was on the alert. The cannoneers sprang to their feet. The long lines emerged from the woods, and moved rapidly but steadily over the fields,

> *They were at once enveloped in a dense cloud of smoke and dust. Arms, heads, blankets, guns and knapsacks were thrown and tossed in to the clear air. . . . A moan went up from the field, distinctly to be heard amid the storm of battle.*
>
> —Lieutenant Colonel Franklin Sawyer, 8th Ohio

toward the Emmitsburg road. Howard's batteries burst into flame, throwing shells with the utmost rapidity. There are gaps in the Rebel ranks, but onward still they come."

Lieutenant Finley of Pickett's Division later wrote, "Still on, steadily on, with the fire growing more furious and deadly, our men advanced . . . as we neared the Emmitsburg Road, the Federals behind the stone fence on the hill opened a rapid fire upon us with muskets . . . Men were falling all around. . . ."

As the Confederates reached the Emmitsburg Road they encountered a strong rail fence lining each side of the lane that could not be pulled down. As the Confederates climbed over the obstacle, the Union defenders fired volley

Brigadier General Lewis Addison Armistead

after volley of musketry into their ranks. Devastated, some rebel units, unable to sustain the terrible losses, began to retreat. Others were cut down in entire rows by **enfilading** artillery fire raining down from Little Round Top and from batteries firing **canister** to their front.

Yet, behind the leading units in the Confederate formation were additional brigades in support. Among these was the brigade led by Lewis Armistead.

At the road, the decimated Confederates returned massed volleys of their own toward the blue coats 200 yards away, both sides enveloped in smoke and fire.

Amid the carnage General Hancock took a bullet to the thigh and was lowered from his horse. A **tourniquet** was applied

High Water Mark—July 3, 1863. Lewis Armistead leads the attack over the stone wall at the Angle.
Illustrated by Don Troiani.

to prevent him from bleeding to death, but he refused evacuation until the battle had been decided.

Not far away, Hancock's best friend, Armistead, his black hat raised upon the tip of his sword, led the survivors of Pickett's Charge the last 200 yards to the wall at the copse of trees. With their ranks decimated by rifle and canister fire, Armistead knew the moment of decision was at hand. Turning to his men, sword raised, he yelled above the deafening roar of battle, "Come forward, Virginians! Come on, boys, we must give them the cold steel! Who will follow me?"

Lieutenant Finley advanced with Armistead and later recalled, "When we were about seventy-five or one hundred yards from that stone wall, some of the men holding it began to break for the rear, when, without orders, save from captains and lieutenants, our line poured a volley or two into them, and then rushed the fence . . . The Federal gunners stood manfully to their guns. I never saw more gallant bearing in any men. They fired their last shots full in our faces and so close that I thought I felt distinctly the flame of the explosion."

With a chilling rebel yell, the Confederates swept over the stone wall and captured the Union battery placed near the Angle driving the defending infantry back from their wall. War correspondent Charles Coffin witnessed the action:

Men fire into each other's faces, not five feet apart. There are bayonet-thrusts, saber-strokes, pistol-shots . . . hand-to-hand contests . . . men going down on their hands and knees, spinning round like tops, throwing out their arms, gulping up blood, falling; legless, armless, headless. There are ghastly heaps of dead men. Seconds are centuries; minutes, ages; but the thin line does not break!

The Rebel column has lost its power. The lines waver. The soldiers of the front rank look round for their supports. They are gone,—fleeing over the field, broken, shattered, thrown into confusion by the remorseless fire from the cemetery and from the cannon on the ridge. The lines have disappeared like a straw in a candle's flame. The ground is thick with dead, and the wounded are like the withered leaves of autumn. Thousands of Rebels throw down their arms and give themselves up as prisoners.

Armistead went down with wounds to his arm and leg just moments after storming the wall. Captured by Union soldiers, he was carried on a blanket to the rear where he was met by Captain Henry Bingham, an officer on Hancock's staff who later wrote to Hancock of the exact exchange:

I dismounted my horse and inquired of the prisoner his name. He replied General Armistead of the Confederate Army. Observing that his suffering was very great I said to him, General,

Three Confederates taken prisoner at Gettysburg posed for this photo a few days after the battle.
Photo credit: Library of Congress.

> *If the men I had the honor to command that day could not take that position, all hell couldn't take it.*
>
> —Major General Isaac Trimble

I am Captain Bingham of General Hancock's staff, and if you have anything valuable in your possession which you desire taken care of, I will take care of it for you.

He then asked me if it was General Winfield S. Hancock and upon my replying in the affirmative, he informed me that you were an old an valued friend of his and he desired for me to say to you, "Tell General Hancock for me that I have done him and done you all an injury which I shall regret the longest day I live." I then obtained his spurs, watch chain, seal and pocketbook. I told the men to take him to the rear to one of the hospitals.

Along the Union line the soldiers knew that they had at last won a decisive victory over their adversary, who had whipped them time and again until this day. Thousands took up the taunting chant, "Fredericksburg! Fredericksburg!" upon the shattered legions of Lee's army as they stumbled back toward Seminary Ridge. The Confederates had suffered over 50 percent casualties, including over 3,000 men taken prisoner. The copse of trees at the Angle would go down in history as the high-water mark of the Confederacy—the farthest advance of their army, and also perhaps the closest the South ever came to winning its independence.

VISIONS OF APPOMATTOX

Lee, watching the disaster unfold from Seminary Ridge, rode out alone to meet the survivors as they streamed back to the trees. Alexander Porter noted, "Lee, as a soldier, must have at this moment have foreseen Appomattox—that he must have realized that he could never again muster so powerful an army, and that for the future he could only delay, but not avert, the failure of his cause." Yet Lee showed no anger, fear, or disappointment of any kind as he reached out to his wounded soldiers and told them, "This has all been my fault." Colonel Fremantle, who witnessed Lee's actions, was awed by his strength of presence and character:

He was engaged in rallying and in encouraging the broken troops, and was riding about a little in front of the wood, quite alone—the whole of his Staff being engaged in a similar manner further to the rear. His face, which is always placid and cheerful, did not show signs of the slightest disappointment, care, or annoyance; he was addressing to every soldier he met a few words of encouragement, such as, "All this will come right in the end: we'll talk it over afterwards; but, in the mean time, all good men must rally."

> *I never saw troops behave more magnificently than Pickett's division of Virginians did today in that grand charge upon the enemy. And if they had been supported as they were to have been,—but, for some reason not fully explained to me, were not—we would have held the position and the day would have been ours.*
>
> —Robert E. Lee

He spoke to all the wounded men that passed him, and the slightly wounded he exhorted "to bind up their hurts and take up a musket" in this emergency. Very few failed to answer his appeal, and I saw many badly wounded men take off their hats and cheer him. He said to me, "This has been a sad day for us, Colonel—a sad day; but we can't expect always to gain victories."

I saw General Wilcox come up to him, and explain, almost crying, the state of his brigade. General Lee immediately shook hands with him and said cheerfully, "Never mind, general, all this has been MY fault— it is I that have lost this fight, and you must help me out of it in the best way you can." In this manner I saw General Lee encourage and reanimate his somewhat dispirited troops, and magnanimously take upon his own shoulders the whole weight of the re- pulse. It was impossible to look at him or to listen to him without feeling the strongest admiration.

Pickett was equally devastated at seeing his proud division cut down before his eyes by enemy fire. When approached by Lee to reform his division he replied, "General Lee—I have no division."

Fearing an enemy counterattack, Lee pulled together his shattered brigades in a defensive line, but the Union troops never came. The Army of the Potomac had suffered equal losses over the past three days of this epic battle and was content to see the rebels go. Lieutenant Haskell had the honor of informing Meade that the day had been won:

General Meade rode up . . . no **bedizened** hero of some holiday review, but he was a plain man, dressed in a serviceable summer suit of dark blue cloth, without badge or ornament, save the shoulder-straps of his grade, and a light, straight sword of a General.. . . . his soft black felt hat was slouched down over his eyes. His face was very white, not pale, and the lines were marked and earnest and full of care. As he arrived near me, coming up the hill, he asked, in a sharp, eager voice: "How is it going here?" "I believe, General, the enemy's attack is repulsed," I answered.

By this time he was on the crest, and when his eye had for an instant swept over the field, taking in just a glance of the whole—the masses of prisoners, the numerous captured flags which the men were derisively flaunting about, the fugitives of the routed enemy, disappearing with the speed of terror in the woods—partly at what I had told him, partly at what he saw, he said, impressively, and his face lighted: "Thank God."

Chapter Six
Aftermath of Battle—"A Strange and Blighted Land"

*Indeed I tremble for my country
when I reflect that God is just . . .*

—Thomas Jefferson

Even before the guns cooled that hot third day of July a new crisis was at hand—the plight of the wounded. Gettysburg was now a manmade disaster **unparalleled** in American history. Over 20,000 men from both sides lay on the fields or crammed into any available shelter. Every church, private home, barn, stable, pigsty, or shed in and around the town was filled with critically wounded and dying men. Thousands of dead soldiers and horses were scattered for miles in the surrounding fields and woods. The wells had all been pumped dry by thirsty soldiers. As the armies separated themselves from combat, a new battle began in earnest—to rescue the survivors of both sides.

Tillie Pierce, along with Mrs. Weikert and her children, had been evacuated earlier that day to a farm down the Taneytown Road near Two Taverns. By late afternoon they realized the sounds of battle were over and decided to make their way back to the Weikert's home. Tillie recounted in her diary:

As we drove along in the cool of the evening, we noticed that everywhere confusion prevailed. Fences were thrown down near and far; knapsacks, blankets and many other articles, lay scattered here and there. The whole country seemed filled with desolation.

Upon reaching the place I fairly shrank back aghast at the awful sight presented. The approaches were crowded with wounded, dying and dead. The air was filled with moanings, and groanings. As we passed on toward the house, we were compelled to pick our steps in order that we might not tread on the prostrate bodies.

When we entered the house we found it also completely filled with the wounded. We hardly knew what to do or where to go. They, however, removed most of the wounded, and thus after a while made room for the family.

As soon as possible, we endeavored to make ourselves useful by rendering assistance in this heartrending state of affairs. I remember that Mrs.

Weikert went through the house, and after searching awhile, brought all the muslin and linen she could spare. This we tore into bandages and gave them to the surgeons, to bind up the poor soldier's wounds.

By this time, amputating benches had been placed about the house. I must have become inured to seeing the terrors of battle, else I could hardly have gazed upon the scenes now presented. I was looking out one of the windows facing the front yard. Near the basement door, and directly underneath the window I was at, stood one of these benches. I saw them lifting the poor men upon it, then the surgeons sawing and cutting off arms and legs, then again probing and picking bullets from the flesh.

Some of the soldiers fairly begged to be taken next, so great was their suffering, and so anxious were they to obtain relief.

To the south of the house, and just outside of the yard, I noticed a pile of limbs higher than the fence. It was a ghastly sight! Gazing upon these, too often the trophies of the amputating bench, I could have no other feeling, than that the whole scene was one of cruel butchery.

Twilight had now fallen; another day had closed; with the soldiers saying, that they believed this day the

Rebels were whipped, but at an awful sacrifice.

LEE RETREATS FOR VIRGINIA

Saturday dawned and quickly the temperature rose as another hot and humid afternoon approached. The two armies were bloodied and battered—like two prize fighters unwilling to continue the contest—and stood a healthy distance from each other across the valley. Lee hoped Meade would attack and give the Confederates a chance to reclaim some measure of victory over the Union army, but Meade knew his shattered brigades were in no condition to advance though they had certainly won a great and decisive victory.

Tillie remembered that day as well: "On the summits, in the valleys, everywhere we heard the soldiers hurrahing for the victory that had been won. The troops on our right,

The Jacob Weikert House where Tillie assisted the doctors and the wounded.
Photo credit: The Gettysburg Daily.

at Culp's Hill, caught up the joyous sound as it came rolling on from the Round Tops on our left, and soon the whole line of blue, rejoiced in the results achieved." Most befitting of all, it was the fourth of July. By afternoon word had come that Vicksburg had surrendered to General Grant's army in Mississippi. It seemed as if the Union victory was complete; that the war might soon be over.

Lee wasted no time in making plans and issuing orders for his wounded army to retreat back through the Cashtown Gap and across the Potomac back into Virginia. The Army of Northern Virginia had lost a major battle, but they were not a defeated army. The prevailing mood of the Confederate troops was that the enemy's superior position had been the key to their undoing on July 3. But some blamed Lee and his officers for making Pickett's Charge in the first place. One was heard to say, "If Old Jack had been here, it wouldn't have been like this."

Brigadier General John Imboden

The time for **recriminations** would come later. The task at hand was one of escape. Lee summoned Brigadier General John Imboden, a cavalry officer whose troopers had been protecting Lee's supply wagons in Chambersburg. Imboden was given command of a wagon train that would take the wounded who could be moved back to Virginia. Lee's troops would follow along a different route. Low on ammunition and with ranks decimated by three days of hard fighting, Lee was in a dangerous situation. To retreat with so many wounded in the face of the enemy would take all his skill as a commanding general. If his army became trapped on the northern side of the Potomac, it could face total destruction if Meade's army attacked.

Around noon, the sky opened and let loose a howling thunderstorm, drenching the wounded who were unable to find shelter and turned the fields of battle into muddy swamps. Major General Carl Schurz remembered, "A heavy rain set in during the day—the usual rain after a battle—and large numbers had to remain unprotected in the open, there being no room left under roof. I saw long rows of men laying under the eaves of the buildings, the water pouring down upon their bodies in streams."

The storm made Imboden's task to command the wagon train of wounded even more difficult. He later wrote, "The very windows of heaven seemed to have opened . . . The deafening roar of the mingled sounds of heaven and earth all around made it almost impossible to communicate orders, and equally difficult to execute them." Around 4:00 PM, the vast column of wagons began to move out. Imboden's orders were to get to Williamsport with all haste. There the men and horses would rest before crossing the Potomac. His 1,200 wagons were filled to capacity with wounded men.

Imboden wrote of the retreat that night:

The column moved rapidly, considering the rough roads and the darkness, and from almost every wagon for many miles issued heart-rending wails

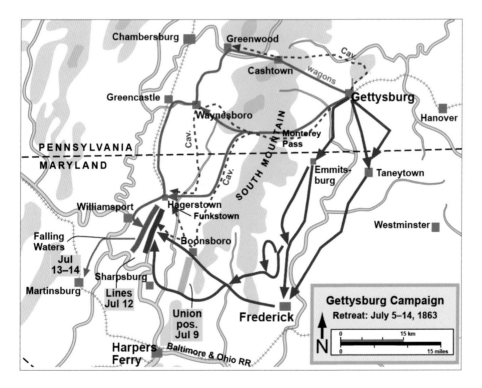

Map by Hal Jespersen, www.cwmaps.com.

A Vast Procession of Misery by Allen Christian Redwood.

of agony . . . Scarcely one in a hundred had received adequate surgical aid, owing to the demands on the hard-working surgeons from still worse cases that had to be left behind . . .

Some were only moaning; some were praying, and others uttering the most fearful oaths and execrations that despair and agony could wring from them; while a majority, with a stoicism sustained by sublime devotion to the cause they fought for, endured without complaint unspeakable tortures, end even spoke words of cheer and comfort to their unhappy comrades of less will or more acute nerves.

No heed could be given to any of their appeals. Mercy and duty to the many forbade the loss of a moment in the vain effort then and there to comply with the prayers of a few. On! On! We must move on.

THE CONFEDERATES WITHDRAW FROM GETTYSBURG

On the night of July 4, Ewell's troops, who were still occupying Gettysburg, quietly prepared to withdraw. The townspeople had heard the massive bombardment and gunfire of the previous afternoon, but no one knew for sure what it all meant. Resident Sarah Broadhead noted the change of mood among the rebel soldiers in her diary: "Who is victorious, or with whom the advantage rests, no one can tell. It would ease the horror if we knew our arms were successful. Some think the Rebels were defeated, as there has been no boasting as on yesterday, and they look uneasy and by no means **exultant**."

Daniel Skelly knew something was afoot and could not sleep that night:

On this night, I went to bed restless and was unable to sleep soundly. About midnight I was awakened by a commotion down in the street. Getting up I went to the window and saw Confederate officers passing through the lines of Confederate soldiers biv-ouacked on the pavement below, telling them to get up quietly and fall back. Very soon the whole line disappeared but we had to remain quietly in our homes for we did not know what it meant.

About 4 AM, there was another commotion in the street, this time on Baltimore, the Fahnestock building being at the corner of West Middle and Baltimore Streets. It seemed to be a noisy demonstration. Going hurriedly to the window I looked out. Ye gods! What a welcome sight for the imprisoned people of Gettysburg! The Boys in Blue marching down the street, fife and drum corps playing, the glorious Stars and Stripes fluttering at the head of the lines.

THE COSTS OF WAR

As Lee's army withdrew toward the Potomac, he surrendered 4,000 wounded men to Union care. The following day, as Meade's army moved out in pursuit of Lee, most of the army doctors went with the troops. Almost overnight, a town of 2,000 residents and a handful of surgeons was left in charge of more than 20,000 wounded men in dire need of care. The task of burying the dead also remained. The devastation—both of people and property—in and around Gettysburg was beyond description.

The bodies of Union soldiers killed during the fighting on July 1, near McPherson's Woods, await burial. Photo credit: Timothy H. O'Sullivan, National Archives.

The Trostle barn near the Peach Orchard after the battle. The dead horses belonged to an artillery battery. Photo credit: National Archives.

The townspeople and volunteers from miles around came to Gettysburg to render aid. The government's Sanitary Commission, an organization similar to today's Red Cross, arrived almost immediately, setting up tents and organizing relief efforts. The wounded were eventually collected into improvised hospitals in tents and buildings where they received medical care until they were well enough to be discharged, moved to a proper hospital, or in the case of the Confederates to prison camps. In these relief efforts the Union wounded received aid first, but once under the care of a doctor, wounded Confederate soldiers were generally treated with the same care as their Union counterparts.

The dead, by necessity, could not receive such tender care. Strewn over miles of the battlefield and lying out for days in the July sun, most of the dead were unrecognizable. Neither army issued "dog tags" or any formal means of identification for the soldiers at that time. Men sometimes sewed their names onto a jacket, or scribbled their names, units, and addresses onto the inside cover of a diary they often carried, but that was the only means of identification at that time. The U.S. government also did not have a formal means of notifying the next of kin that a man had fallen in battle, so many men simply disappeared, buried in mass graves with others from their unit wherever they were killed on a battlefield.

The graves of Confederate soldiers await completion after the battle. Photo credit: Timothy H. O'Sullivan, Library of Congress.

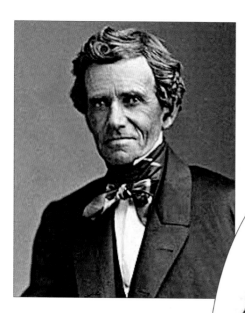

Samuel Wilkeson of the New York Times.

Lieutenant Bayard Wilkeson

there spread out before us was terrible to contemplate! Dead soldiers, bloated horses, shattered cannon and **caissons**, thousands of small arms. In fact everything . . . was there in one confused and indescribable mass."

Daniel walked to the Round Tops from town the following day and noted that "the whole countryside was covered with ruins of the battle. One of the saddest sights of the day's visit on the field I witnessed near the Devil's Den, on the low ground in that vicinity. There were twenty-six Confederate officers, ranking from a colonel to lieutenants, laid side by side in a row for burial. At the head of each was a board giving their names, ranks and commands to which they belonged . . . They had evidently been prepared for burial by their Confederate companions before they had fallen back, so that their identity would be preserved, and they would receive a respectable burial."

Tillie and Daniel were witness to the devastation wrought upon their quiet town following the battle. Tillie ventured out with her friend Beckie Weikert on July 5, escorted by an army lieutenant, to visit the summit of Little Round Top: "As we stood upon those mighty boulders, and looked down into the chasms between, we beheld the dead lying there just as they had fallen during the struggle. From the summit of Little Round Top, surrounded by the wrecks of battle, we gazed upon the valley of death beneath. The view

Among the masses of people heading toward Gettysburg after the battle were relatives of soldiers coming to search for their loved ones while there was still time. One such search immediately gripped the nation. Sam Wilkeson, a war correspondent for the *New York Times*, had arrived at Gettysburg on July 2, to report on the epic battle. Both of his sons were in the Union army, including Lieutenant Bayard Wilkeson of Battery G, 4th U.S. Artillery. This unit had been overrun at Barlow's Knoll on the first day's fighting, covering the retreat of the Eleventh Corps. Learning that his son had been killed in action Sam Wilkeson went to look for him after the battle had ceased.

Finding his son's mangled corpse and learning of the desperate circumstances of his death, Sam Wilkeson sat next to the body and wrote an angry dispatch to his paper: "Who can write the history of a battle whose eyes are immovably fastened upon a central figure of **transcendingly** absorbing interest— the dead body of an oldest born son, crushed by a shell in a position where a battery should never have been sent, and abandoned to death in a building where surgeons dared not to stay." His writing touched the hearts of millions.

THE UNKNOWN SOLDIER OF GETTYSBURG

As the Gettysburg townspeople began burying the dead, the body of a Union soldier was discovered tucked off a street where he had crawled, mortally wounded, to die. His jacket had no badges, no signs of rank or unit, and his pockets contained nothing to identify him—no letters or diary. Yet in his hand he grasped a small photo of three young children. The last act of his life had been to gaze upon their faces.

The photo came into the possession of Dr. J. Francis Bourns, a Philadelphia doctor on his way to help the wounded from the battlefield. He hoped to locate the mother of the children in the photograph by publishing a detailed description of them in all the local papers. A major story ran in the *Philadelphia Inquirer* on October 19, 1863, entitled, "Whose Father Was He?" As the story grew in fame and as the photo of the children was printed onto thousands of small post cards, the nation waited in suspense. Would anyone identify the children?

Dr. Bourns soon received a letter from a woman in Portville, New York, who had not heard from her husband since the battle of Gettysburg. She requested a copy of the photograph. When she received it in the mail she looked upon the faces of her three children—Franklin, Alice, and Frederick—who were now fatherless. The woman's name was Phylinda Humiston. Her fallen husband was Sergeant Amos Humiston of Company C, 154th New York Volunteers. Sergeant Humiston came to symbolize the thousands of missing men at Gettysburg and other battles, whose widows and orphaned children waited for them in vain.

Sergeant Amos Humiston

"The Children of the Battlefield,"
later identified as Frank, Frederick,
and Alice Humiston.

To My Wife

You have put the little ones to bed dear
  wife
And covered them over with care
My Frankey Alley and Fred
And they have said their evening prayer

Perhaps they breathed the name of one
Who is far in southern land
And wished he too were there
To join their little band

I am very sad to tonight dear wife
My thoughts are dwelling on home and
  thee
As I keep the lone night watch
Beneath the holly tree

The winds are sighing through the trees
And as they onward roam
They whisper hopes of happiness
Within our cottage home

And as they onward passed
Over hill and vale and bubbling stream
They wake up thoughts within my soul
Like music in a dream

Oh when will this rebellion cease
This cursed war be over
And we our dear ones meet
To part from them no more?

—Amos Humiston, March 25th 1863

Three years after the battle, an orphanage was established at Gettysburg—called The Homestead Association—for the benefit of children whose fathers had been killed in the service of their country. Mrs. Humiston and her children were among the first to reside at the home. James Garfield, future president of the United States, was on the board of trustees. Dr. Bourns served as the first general secretary. The founding of the orphanage was reported nationwide for a citizenry still trying to understand the meaning of the great sacrifices made during the Civil War.

TILLIE RETURNS HOME

Amid all the human agony and loss during those first days of July 1863, there was at least one happy homecoming as Tillie Pierce made her way back to Gettysburg and to her father's house on Baltimore Street:

> Sometime during the forenoon of Tuesday, the 7th, in company with Mrs. Schriver and her two children, I started off on foot to reach my home.
>
> As it was impossible to travel the roads, on account of the mud, we took to the fields. While passing along, the stench arising from the fields of carnage was most sickening. Dead horses, swollen to almost twice their natural size, lay in all directions, stains of blood frequently met our gaze, and all kinds of army accoutrements covered the ground. Fences had disappeared, some buildings were gone, others ruined. The whole landscape had been changed, and I felt as though we were in a strange and blighted land.
>
> I hastened into the house. Everything seemed to be in confusion, and my home did not look exactly as it did when I left. Large bundles had been prepared, and were lying around in different parts of the room I had entered. They had expected to be compelled to leave the town suddenly. I soon found my mother and the rest. At first glance even my mother did not recognize me, so dilapidated was my general appearance. The only clothes I had along had by this time become covered with mud, the greater part of which was gathered the day on which we left home.
>
> As soon as I spoke my mother ran to me, and clasping me in her arms, said: "Why, my dear child, is that you? How glad I am to have you home again without any harm having befallen you!"

DANIEL BECOMES AN ENTREPRENEUR

Daniel and his friends realized the aftermath of the great battle would be one of a more businesslike opportunity as around 60,000 new

143

customers were camped within the Union lines just outside town:

> *My friend "Gus" Bentley met me on the street and told me that down at the Hollinger warehouse where he was employed they had a lot of tobacco. "We hid it away before the Rebs came into town," he continued, "and they did not find it. We can buy it and take it out and sell it to the soldiers." Like all boys of those days we had little spending money but we concluded we would try and raise the cash in some way.*
>
> *I went to my mother and consulted her about it and she loaned me ten dollars. Gus also got ten, all of which we invested in the tobacco. It was in large plugs—Congress tobacco, a well known brand at that time. With an old-fashioned tobacco cutter we cut it up into ten cent pieces and each of us took a basket full and started out Baltimore Street to the cemetery, the nearest line of battle.*
>
> *The soldiers helped us over the breastworks with our baskets and in a short time they were empty and our pockets filled with ten-cent pieces. The soldiers told us to go home and get some more tobacco, that they would buy all we could bring out. We made a number of trips, selling out each time, and after disposing of all our supply, and paying back our borrowed capital, we each had more money than we ever had before in our lives.*

Young Daniel would play an even more important role in the recovery efforts in the following weeks, though:

> *In the days following the battle, the firm of Fahnestock Brothers received numerous inquires about wounded soldiers who were scattered over the field in the hospitals hastily set up at points most conveniently located to take care of the casualties. With Mrs. E. G. Fahnestock, I frequently rode back and forth among these stations, either in buggy or on horseback, looking for wounded men about whom information was sought. Sometimes it was difficult to locate them. We made other trips to the hospitals in the college and seminary buildings also. Frequently on these trips were included supplies of delicacies for the men. So it was that the people of Gettysburg assisted in every way in solving the problems that arose incident to the great battle.*

The Plan for a National Cemetery

Plans for a national cemetery for the Union dead were put into action soon after the battle.

Pennsylvania Governor Andrew Curtin ordered his agent, attorney David Wills, to acquire the Evergreen Cemetery and its surrounding land as a final resting place for more than 3,000 Union soldiers. William Saunders, a famous landscape architect, was **commissioned** to design the cemetery. He placed the fallen in rows of sweeping arcs, giving each state equal prominence. In early November,

Pennsylvania Governor Andrew Curtin. Photo credit: Matthew Brady, Library of Congress.

Union remains were transferred from their original burial sites to the graves within the cemetery.

A dedication for the Soldiers National Cemetery was planned for November 19, 1863, and David Wills invited the statesman Edward Everett, a premier orator of that time, to give the **keynote** speech. Only three weeks before the dedication, Wills also invited President Lincoln

David Wills

William Saunders

Abraham reading to his son Tad.
Photo credit: Library of Congress.

during a war that was growing increasingly unpopular.

Gettysburg had been an opportunity to end the war, yet Lee had escaped over the Potomac back to Virginia and safety. The war and the endless suffering of millions continued. A **distraught** Lincoln had blamed Meade (perhaps unfairly) after the battle and told Secretary Hay,

William Wallace "Willie" Lincoln

Army officer E. W. Andrews, who traveled with Lincoln that day, remembered that "during the ride to Gettysburg the president placed everyone who approached him at his ease, relating numerous stories, some of them laughable, and others of a character that deeply touched the hearts of his listeners." But behind the lighthearted conversations, Lincoln was under the immense pressures of his duties as president

"Our Army held the war in the hollow of their hand and they would not close it." With Lee's army still successfully defending Richmond, however, Lincoln faced the real possibility that the American people would lose the will to see the war through to victory.

Now Lincoln would be making a speech at a dedication of the final resting place for thousands of his soldiers who had fallen at Gettysburg. Many people in the North were calling for an end to the war, supporting Lincoln's political rival George C. McClellan to form a new administration in 1864, to negotiate peace with the Confederacy. If that happened, everything Lincoln had worked for—the preservation of the union, the abolishment of slavery, and the sacrifices of millions of people—would have been in vain.

Mary Todd Lincoln.
Photo credit: Matthew Brady,
Library of Congress.

He comes to me every night, and stands at the foot of my bed with the same sweet, adorable smile he has always had; he does not always come alone; little Eddie is sometimes with him . . . You cannot dream of the comfort this gives me. When I thought of my little son in immensity, alone, without his mother to direct him, no one to hold his little hand in loving guidance, it nearly broke my heart.

—Mary Todd Lincoln

149

Foremost among his thoughts that day, though, must have been for his ten-year-old son Tad. Only a year earlier, in February 1862, Tad and his older brother William had contracted **typhoid fever** while living at the White House. Tad survived the ordeal, but William did not. His death was a devastating loss to the President and his wife, who had already lost their second son Edward when he was only four years old, in 1850. In her grief, Mary Todd was pushed beyond the limits of her sanity and never fully recovered.

William's death also pushed Lincoln into a deep depression that he kept hidden from most. Hay wrote that the president "was profoundly moved by [William's] death, though he gave no outward sign of his trouble, but kept about his work the same as ever. His bereaved heart seemed afterwards to pour out its fullness on his youngest child." The great pressures of his official duties, the loss of his son, and the worsening instability of his wife inspired Lincoln into a closer relationship with God. His letters and speeches increasingly revealed that Lincoln turned to his faith for guidance.

A year earlier Lincoln had written to a friend, Eliza Gurney, that "If I had had my way, this war would never have been **commenced**; if I had been allowed my way, this war would have ended before this, but we find it still continues; and we must believe that He permits it for some wise purpose of his own, mysterious and unknown to us; and though with our limited understandings we may not be able to **comprehend** it, yet we cannot but believe that He who made the world still governs it."

Lincoln knew there was a great weariness among the people. The Confederacy showed no signs of surrendering their cause for independence. Lincoln knew what he was asking by continuing the war: The deaths from battle and disease, the orphaned children and widowed mothers, the total destruction of land and property—Americans slaughtering Americans—would continue.

Lincoln also knew what pain and suffering meant. He knew what it was like to lose a son. But with the future of the country at stake and with a chance to end slavery, Lincoln would not accept a compromised peace. A year earlier he had written to William Seward, "I expect to maintain this contest until successful, or till I die, or am conquered, or my term expires, or Congress or the country **forsakes** me."

There is a legend that Lincoln jotted down his Gettysburg speech on the back of an envelope on the train the day of the dedication. That, of course, is simply a tall tale. He had known about the invitation to speak at the dedication of the cemetery for some time. Lincoln was a master of the

Lincoln and Slavery

By 1863, Lincoln most certainly viewed his own role in events not only as the protector of the union, but the instrument by which the United States could rid itself of the curse of slavery. On January 1 of that year, Lincoln had legally freed all Confederate-held slaves with the Emancipation Proclamation.

Emancipation of the slaves was made as an executive order using Lincoln's wartime powers as Commander in Chief of the armed forces, and thus it did not have to be passed by Congress. It was a measure Lincoln took to help bring an end to the war, but it also neatly served his personal belief, and the belief of many other Americans, that all men, everywhere, should be free. Lincoln explained this in a special message to Congress in December 1862: "Fellow-citizens, we cannot escape history . . . In giving freedom to the slave, we assure freedom to the free—honorable alike in what we give, and what we preserve. We shall nobly save, or meanly lose, the last best hope of earth."

Ironically, the war fought by the Confederacy to preserve slavery became the legal means by which Lincoln was able to free them and eventually banish slavery from the United States with the Thirteenth Amendment. Until that momentous and courageous act of emancipation had been taken, slaves were simply the legal property of American citizens, protected by the Constitution—the very Constitution Lincoln had sworn to defend taking the oath to become President. Slavery in America, a country founded on the **premise** that all men are created equal, was hypocrisy of the worst kind. Slavery had divided the nation for decades and became the single issue over which Americans could find no compromise. Lincoln knew slavery had to be ended in order for the nation to be truly united.

English language and he would craft his speeches and letters with painstaking care, often making several drafts and asking those closest to him for their advice. This speech, though, he kept to himself, only asking William Seward to review it with him the evening before the dedication ceremony. Lincoln knew he would be speaking after a long oration by Edward Everett and had kept his comments to just a few words. The speech, written on a few loose papers, was kept in his pocket.

Lincoln and his staff arrived at Gettysburg around 6:00 PM. The town was in celebration over the upcoming event. Ten thousand visitors crammed the town, bands were playing, crowds were cheering and singing, and everyone was anxious for a glimpse of the president. Lincoln and the other dignitaries went to David Wills's house at the center of town, where they dined and where Lincoln stayed the night. The president made a brief appearance to wave to the amassed crowd and

Edward Everett

to say a few words, but he made no formal **oration**. That night he stayed up in his room late into the evening, working on his speech.

The next morning, at 10:00 AM, Lincoln met with the other dignitaries who had come far and wide to witness the dedication. Principle among them was Andrew Curtin, the Governor of Pennsylvania. They made up a large procession, and Lincoln road slowly on horseback, covering the mile walk from the center of town to the new cemetery on the ridge, adjacent to the old Evergreen Cemetery that had been at the center of the battle. Thousands of people lined the way on either side of the road.

A Gettysburg resident wrote that Lincoln bowed "with a modest smile and uncovered head to the throng of women, men and children that greeted him from the doors and windows." Near the cemetery the scars of battle were still readily apparent; "all about were traces of the fierce conflict. Rifle pits, cut and scarred trees, broken fences, pieces of artillery wagons and harness, scraps of blue and gray clothing, bent canteens . . ." It was a stark reminder about the cost of victory at Gettysburg—over 3,500 Northern soldiers would eventually be buried where they now stood.

The dedication opened with a prayer and then Everett's speech, which had been billed as the primary oration for the event; Lincoln would then follow with his remarks. The day was cloudy but without rain, and warm for November. Everett rose and began: "STAND-ING beneath this serene sky, overlooking these broad fields now reposing from the labors of the waning year, the mighty Alleghenies dimly towering before us, the graves of our brethren beneath our feet, it is with hesitation that I raise my poor voice to break the eloquent silence of God and Nature . . ."

For the next two hours Everett spoke with great **eloquence**, recalling the events of the campaign and the battle fought at Gettysburg. This is what people had come to hear—one of the greatest speakers of his time delivering an epic story of the battle's events. There was much applause when he finished and the band played as everyone congratulated Everett.

Now it was Lincoln's turn to speak. The crowd quieted and waited. Lincoln, still seated, took a few small papers from his pocket, found one and read it carefully, then returned it to his coat. This was not a speech to be read aloud from notes, but to be given from the soul.

George D. Gitt, who saw Lincoln that morning, recorded that "tucking away the papers, he arose, and very slowly stepped to the front of the platform. The flutter and motion of the crowd ceased the moment the president was on his feet. Such was the quiet that his footfalls . . . woke echoes, and with the creak-ing of the boards, it was as if someone were walking through the hallways of an empty house."

E. W. Andrews recalled that Lincoln "came out before the vast assembly, and stepped slowly to the front of the platform, with his hands clasped before him, his natural sadness of expression deepened, his head bent forward, and his eyes cast to the ground. In this attitude he stood for a few seconds, si-lent, as if communing with his own thoughts; and when he began to speak, and through-out his entire address, his manner indicated no consciousness of the presence of tens of thousands hanging on his lips, but rather of one who, like the prophet of old, was over-mastered by some unseen spirit of the scene, and passively gave utterance to the memories, the feelings, the **counsels** and the **prophecies** with which he was inspired." He spoke these simple words:

Four score and seven years ago our fathers brought forth on this continent a new nation, conceived in liberty, and dedicated to the proposition that all men are created equal. Now we are engaged in a great civil war, testing whether that nation, or any nation, so conceived and so dedicated, can long endure. We are met on a great battle-field of that war. We have come to dedicate a portion of that field, as a final resting place for those who here gave their lives that that nation might live. It is altogether fitting and proper that we should do this.

But, in a larger sense, we can not dedicate, we can not consecrate, we can not hallow this ground. The brave men, living and dead, who struggled here, have consecrated it, far above our poor power to add or detract. The world will little note, nor long remember what we say here, but it can never forget what they did here. It is for us the living, rather, to be dedicated here to the unfinished work which they who fought here have thus far so nobly advanced. It is rather for us to be here dedicated to the great task remaining before us — that from these honored dead we take increased devotion to that cause for which they gave the last full measure of devotion — that we here highly resolve that these dead shall not have died in vain — that this nation, under God, shall have a new birth of freedom — and that government of the people, by the people, for the people, shall not perish from the earth.

The **brevity** of Lincoln's words surprised the crowd. Many stood silent at his conclusion, transfixed by his words. Gitt recalled, "Had not Lincoln turned and moved toward his chair, the audience would very likely have remained voiceless for several moments more. Finally there came applause and a calling, 'Yes! Yes! Government for the people!' It was as if the Blue Ridge Mountains to the west were echoing Lincoln's concluding and keynote thought." Three cheers erupted for the president and his delegation.

Many newspapers reported the event according to the political allegiances. The *Chicago Times* reported that Lincoln's words were "silly, flat and dish-watery utterances."

Lincoln's address at the dedication of the Gettysburg National Cemetery, November 19, 1863. Image credit: Library of Congress.

Massachusetts' *Springfield Republican* called the address "a perfect gem, deep in feeling, compact in thought and expression," and *Harper's Weekly* commented, "The few words of the President were from the heart to the heart."

Of all the compliments he received, though, the one that pleased Lincoln the most came from a friend and political supporter: Edward Everett. Everett wrote to Lincoln the day after the dedication: "Permit me also to express my great admiration of the thoughts expressed by you, with such eloquent simplicity and appropriateness, at the consecration of the Cemetery. I should be glad, if I could flatter myself that I came as near to the central idea of the occasion, in two hours, as you did in two minutes."

History would come to agree with Everett. In just two minutes, Lincoln had reminded Americans that the nation was founded on the principles of human equality expressed by the Declaration of Independence. The war was a struggle to preserve the nation and democracy as envisioned by the founding fathers. It was now up to the country to dedicate itself to achieving a final victory over the Confederacy so that the thousands who perished at Gettysburg had not sacrificed their lives in vain. Such a victory would grant America a new birth of freedom, a new nation without slavery—one nation, indivisible, whose government was dedicated to the freedom and rights of all its people.

Lincoln's words have lasted throughout time and are now a deep part of our American culture. More than words simply carved into the stone blocks of the Lincoln Memorial in Washington, DC, the Gettysburg Address lives on. Lincoln's words remind us what it means to be an American—what America aspires to as a nation. His words are a living legacy to our cherished rights and freedoms linking our past to the future. Lincoln spoke of those darkest days of the Civil War as a great struggle in our quest to secure freedom for all, a quest that still continues to this day.

Lincoln greeting people just after his Gettysburg Address. Photo credit: National Archives.

Charles Sumner, a senator and **abolitionist** from Massachusetts, writing just after Lincoln's assassination in 1865, noted "that speech, uttered at the field of Gettysburg . . . and now sanctified by the martyrdom of its author, is a monumental act. In the modesty of his nature he said 'the world will little note, nor long remember what we say here; but it can never forget what they did here.' He was mistaken. The world at once noted what he said, and will never cease to remember it. The battle itself was less important than the speech. Ideas are always more than battles."

MARTIN LUTHER KING, JR.
QUOTES LINCOLN'S GETTYSBURG ADDRESS

A century after Gettysburg, on August 18, 1963, another great American, Martin Luther King, Jr., would stand on the steps of the Lincoln memorial in front of over 200,000 people and quote from Lincoln's Gettysburg Address is his opening words: "Five score years ago, a great American, in whose symbolic shadow we stand today, signed the Emancipation Proclamation. This momentous decree

came as a great beacon light of hope to millions of Negro slaves who had been seared in the flames of **withering** injustice." In his epic "I Have a Dream" speech, King appealed for civil equality, "I have a dream, that my four little children will one day live in a nation where they will not be judged by the color of their skin but by the content of their character. I have a dream today!"

Epilogue

*Through our great good fortune, in our youth
our hearts were touched with fire.*

—Oliver Wendell Holmes, Jr.

On October 3, 1888, Joshua Lawrence Chamberlain and the survivors of the 20th Maine gathered around a large granite monument being dedicated to the memory of their regiment. Chamberlain, now sixty years old, spoke with great eloquence on what the battlefield had come to mean for the nation:

*The 20th Maine Reunion, 1889. Joshua Chamberlain is seated at center right.
Photo credit: Maine Historical Society.*

Here the 20th Maine Regiment Col. J. L. Chamberlain Commanding.
Forming the Extreme Left of the National Line of Battle.
On the 2nd Day of July, 1863. Repulsed the Attack of the Extreme Right
of Longstreet's Corps. and Charged in Turn, Capturing 308 Prisoners.
The Regiment Lost 38 Killed or Mortally Wounded,
and 93 Wounded Out of 358 Engaged.
This Monument Erected By Survivors of the Regiment.
A.D. 1888. Marks Very Nearly the Spot Where Colors Stood

The 20th Maine Infantry Memorial on Little Round Top.
Photo credit: Jen Goellnitz.

In great deeds, something abides. On great fields, something stays. Forms change and pass; bodies disappear; but spirits linger, to consecrate ground for the vision-place of souls. And reverent men and women from afar, and generations that know us not and that we know not of, heart-drawn to see where and by whom great things were suffered and done for them, shall come to this deathless field, to ponder and dream; and lo! the shadow of a mighty presence shall wrap them in its bosom, and the power of the vision pass into their souls.

The battlefield at Gettysburg had become a sacred place to all Americans. In 1864, a group of citizens established the Gettysburg Memorial

Association, which was dedicated to preserving the battlefield as a memorial to the Union army. In 1895, the land holdings were transferred to the Federal Government, which designated Gettysburg as a National Military Park. It became a memorial to both armies as veterans from either side eventually came and dedicated monuments to the memory of their troops' heroic deeds in July 1863. The administration of the park was transferred to the Department of the Interior's National Park Service in 1933, which continues to this day.

Gettysburg eventually became hallowed ground where both sides came to find peace, and in time, to **reconcile** with former enemies. Two grand reunions were held there, the first in 1913 to commemorate the fiftieth anniversary of the battle. It was the largest Civil War reunion ever held with over 53,000 veterans in attendance. President Woodrow Wilson expressed the mood of the occasion in his July 4, 1913 speech: "We have found one another again as brothers and comrades in arms, enemies no longer, generous friends rather, our battles long past, the quarrel forgotten—except that we shall not forget the splendid valor."

The second reunion was held in 1933 to mark the seventy-fifth anniversary of

Union and Confederate veterans meet as friends at the fiftieth anniversary of the battle in 1913. Photo credit: Library of Congress.

Some of the last surviving veterans of the Gettysburg battle shake hands over the stone wall at the Angle during the seventy-fifth anniversary in 1933. Photo credit: National Archives.

the battle. Now in their nineties, the last of the veterans came for one final visit to their sacred field. President Franklin Roosevelt spoke at the dedication of the Eternal Light Peace Memorial on July 3 of that year, noting, "Surely, all this is holy ground . . . Here, at Gettysburg, here in the presence of the spirits of those who fell on this ground, we give renewed assurance that the passions of war are moldering in the tombs of Time and the purposes of peace are flowing today in the hearts of a united people."

Gettysburg is the best preserved battlefield of the Civil War today and rightfully so. Over a million visitors each year travel to the site of the battle "to ponder and dream" as Chamberlain so perfectly foretold. If the Civil War is considered the crossroads of the American soul, then Gettysburg is surely the spiritual center of that experience for both North and South. For this author, the battlefield remains a stark reminder of the great sacrifices of both sides—a testament to the courage and loyalty of the American character—and of the cost of forging a nation dedicated to its ideal that all men are created equal. The Battle of Gettysburg and Lincoln's speech are timeless reminders from our epic past of what it truly means to be an American.

Postscript

The Civilians

Matilda "Tillie" Pierce married Horace Alleman, a lawyer who graduated from Gettysburg College, and moved with him to Selinsgrove, Pennsylvania, where they stayed the rest of their lives and raised three children. Her memoir, *At Gettysburg: Or What A Girl Saw And Heard Of The Battle*, was published in 1889. She passed away in 1914, and is buried in the Trinity Lutheran Cemetery at Selinsgrove.

Daniel A. Skelly remained in Gettysburg his whole life, eventually rising from store clerk to a partner of the Fahnestock dry goods store. His memoir, *A Boy's Experiences During the Battle of Gettysburg*, was published in 1932, at the urging of his family, just a few months before he passed away. He is buried at Evergreen Cemetery in Gettysburg.

Mary Virginia "Ginnie" Wade was laid to rest at Evergreen Cemetery in Gettysburg. When Lincoln spoke at Gettysburg on November 19, her sister, Georgia McClellan, was seated near the president. A monument, dedicated at her grave in 1900, flies the American flag overhead around the clock. She is only one of two American women so honored. She was the only Gettysburg civilian killed during the battle.

Elizabeth Salome "Sallie" Myers remained in Gettysburg and married Henry Stewart in 1867. Henry was the brother of Sergeant Alexander Stewart, the mortally wounded soldier she had helped while serving as a nurse. She had written to Henry about his brother's death, and they met when he came to Gettysburg. She gave birth to one son, who eventually became a doctor and preserved her diary. Her account, *How A Gettysburg Schoolteacher Spent Her Vacation in 1863*, was published in 1903. She passed away in 1922, and is buried at Evergreen Cemetery in Gettysburg.

The Army of the Potomac

Corporal Johnston Hastings Skelly died of his wounds received in the battle of Winchester on

June 26, 1863. He is buried 100 feet from his betrothed, Mary Virginia Wade, at Evergreen Cemetery in Gettysburg.

Lieutenant Franklin Aretas Haskell wrote his account of Gettysburg in a letter to his brother two weeks after the event, which was later published in 1898, as *The Battle of Gettysburg*. Bruce Catton proclaimed Haskell's writing as "one of the genuine classics of Civil War literature." On February 9, 1864, Haskell was appointed colonel of the 36th Wisconsin. On June 3, he assumed command of the 1st Brigade, 2nd Division, Second Corps when its commander, Colonel Henry Boyd McKeen, was killed during the Battle of Cold Harbor. Shortly after taking command he was shot through the temple and killed while leading a charge.

Colonel Régis de Trobriand was promoted to Major General by the end of the war. He remained in the army, serving in the Dakota territories and later in New Orleans during reconstruction. He published a book, *Four Years with the Army of the Potomac*, in 1889, and passed away at the age of eight-one in 1897. He is buried at St. Ann's Episcopal Cemetery in Sayville, New York.

Colonel Joshua Lawrence Chamberlain was relieved from command after Gettysburg to recover from malaria and dysentery. He returned to command a brigade at the Siege of Petersburg, where he was nearly killed by a round through the hip and groin. Presumed to be dying, General Grant promoted Chamberlain to Brigadier General. Surviving against all odds, Chamberlain recovered and took command of the 1st Brigade of the 1st Division of Fifth Corps, who he fought with during Grant's last advance toward Appomattox. Wounded a second time, Chamberlain was brevetted to the rank of major general by President Abraham Lincoln. He presided over the final parade of the Army of Northern Virginia at their surrender at Appomattox in April 1865. He would go on to serve four terms as governor of Maine after the war. He passed away in 1914 at the age of eighty-five and is buried in Pine Grove Cemetery in Brunswick, Maine.

Reverend William Corby went on to serve two terms as president of the University of Notre Dame. The school's Corby Hall is named for him. There is a statue dedicated to Corby at Gettysburg memorializing his general absolution to the Irish Brigade on the second day of the battle. He also wrote *Memoirs of Chaplain Life: Three Years with the Irish Brigade in the Army of the Potomac*. He passed away in 1897.

Lieutenant Colonel Rufus Dawes returned to Ohio and married his fiancé Mary Beman Gates in January 1864. He fought again at the Battle of the Wilderness and at the Siege of Petersburg. In July 1864, Dawes declined the promotion to colonel and mustered out of the army. In honor of his service, he was brevetted as a brigadier general of volunteers by President Andrew Johnson in 1866. Dawes returned to Marietta, Ohio, and entered business. He would serve a single term in the U.S. House of Representatives in 1881. His memoir, *Service with the 6th Wisconsin Volunteers,* was published in 1890. Dawes passed away in 1899, at the age of sixty-one in Marietta, Ohio, and is buried in Oak Grove Cemetery. His son, Charles G. Dawes, served as vice president of the United States under Calvin Coolidge.

Brigadier General John Buford fought with his cavalry through the remainder of 1863, but fell ill in December possibly from typhoid fever. Resting at a friend's home in Washington, DC, Lincoln was informed the general was dying and promoted him to major general "for distinguished and meritorious service at the Battle of Gettysburg." He died on December 16, 1863.

Brigadier General George Armstrong Custer was promoted to command a cavalry division and fought through all of the 1864–1865 campaign to Appomattox. After the war, Custer went on to lead the 7th Cavalry Regiment in the Great Sioux War of 1876. At the Battle of the Little Big Horn on June 25, 1876, in the Montana Territory, Custer and over 200 of his soldiers were surrounded and killed by warriors from three different Indian tribes.

Major General Daniel Sickles survived the amputation of his right leg and recuperated in Washington, DC, where he was visited by President Lincoln after the battle. Sickles was not charged with insubordination for moving his corps forward at Gettysburg on July 2, and became a dedicated enemy of Gordon Meade. Sickles claimed that victory at Gettysburg had been possible because of his actions and that Meade had secretly planned to withdraw the army. True to his nature and political connections, Sickles lobbied to have himself awarded the Medal of Honor, which he eventually received thirty-four years later. His leg bone was preserved by the Army Surgeon General as a wartime injury specimen and can be seen today at the National Museum of Health and Medicine. Sickles passed away in New York City in 1914 at the age of ninety-four and is buried at Arlington National Cemetery.

Major General Winfield Scott Hancock survived the wound to his right thigh and returned to command the Second Corps in the 1864 Battle of the Wilderness, Battle of Spotsylvania Courthouse and Cold Harbor, and the Siege of Petersburg. Hancock was promoted to brigadier general in the regular army after that. In 1865, Hancock was assigned to supervise the execution of the Lincoln assassination conspirators. In 1880, Hancock lost in a presidential bid against James A. Garfield. He passed away in 1886 at Governors Island and is buried in Montgomery Cemetery near Norristown, Pennsylvania.

Major General George Gordon Meade was promoted to Brigadier General in the regular army and received the Thanks of Congress for his victory at Gettysburg. He would retain command of the Army of the Potomac for the rest of the war, serving under Ulysses S. Grant and fighting inconclusive battles against Lee's fixed defenses in the 1864 campaign. Meade passed away in Philadelphia at the age of fifty-six in 1872, and is buried at Laurel Hill Cemetery.

The Army of Northern Virginia

Private Wesley Culp was killed fighting with the 2nd Virginia Infantry on his uncle's land at Culp's Hill on July 2. He was buried by members of his unit, but the gravesite was lost to time. In his pocket was the last letter from Johnston Skelly to Mary Virginia Wade, who never knew the fate of her fiancé before she was killed the following day.

Colonel William Calvin Oates went on to fight again at Chickamauga, at the Battle of the Wilderness and at the Battle of Spotsylvania Courthouse. Promoted to Brigadier General and given command of the 48th Alabama Regiment, we was badly wounded in the siege of Petersburg and lost his right arm. After the war, Oates returned to his law practice and was eventually elected in 1880 to the U.S. House of Representatives, where he served seven consecutive terms. He was elected as Governor of Alabama in 1894. Oates passed away in Montgomery, Alabama, in 1910, at the age of seventy-four and is buried in Oakwood Cemetery.

Brigadier General Lewis Addison Armistead died of his wounds at a Federal hospital on July 5. Lewis Armistead is buried next to his uncle, Lieutenant Colonel George Armistead, commander of the garrison of Fort McHenry during the Battle of Baltimore, at the Old Saint Paul's Cemetery in Baltimore, Maryland.

Major General James Ewell Brown Stuart fought valiantly on July 3 against Union cavalry and brilliantly defended Lee's retreat to the Potomac in the following weeks. He was mortally wounded the following year on May 11, 1864, at Yellow Tavern, Virginia. One of the true Confederate heroes and among the best cavalry leaders, Gettysburg was the only serious blemish on his legendary career.

Lieutenant General Richard Stoddert Ewell fought with his corps again in May 1864, in both the Battle of the Wilderness and the Battle of Spotsylvania Court House. Due to lingering effects of his wartime injuries and combat fatigue, Lee assigned Ewell to command the garrison of the Department of Richmond. After

> "So far from engaging in a war to perpetuate slavery, I am
> rejoiced that Slavery is abolished. I believe it will be greatly
> for the interest of the South. So fully am I satisfied of this that
> I would have cheerfully lost all that I have lost by the war, and
> have suffered all that I have suffered to have this object attained."
>
> —Robert E. Lee, May 1, 1870

the war, Ewell retired to work as a "gentleman farmer" on his wife's farm near Spring Hill, Tennessee. He passed away in 1872 at the age of fifty-four and is buried in Old City Cemetery in Nashville, Tennessee.

Lieutenant General Ambrose Powell Hill, Jr. fought with his Third Corps in the 1864 campaign in the Battles of the Wilderness and Spotsylvania Courthouse, Cold Harbor, and finally at the Siege of Petersburg. He was killed by an enemy sharpshooter on April 2, 1865, as he rode along the lines at Petersburg. He is buried in Richmond, Virginia.

Lieutenant General James Longstreet remained in command of his First Corps and fought brilliantly at the Battle of the Wilderness, where he was badly wounded by a round

through the shoulder. He recuperated in time to command the defenses of Richmond and retreated with Lee to Appomattox where they surrendered to Longstreet's close friend, Ulysses S. Grant. After the war, Longstreet settled in New Orleans, where he entered business and later moved to Gainesville, Georgia. Longstreet was the only Confederate general to join the Republican Party in the years after the Civil War, supporting Ulysses S. Grant's run for the presidency in 1868. Often blamed for failing Lee at Gettysburg, Longstreet became a scapegoat for the "Lost Cause" of the Confederacy by those who wished to defend Lee's reputation. Longstreet published his memoir, *From Manassas to Appomattox,* in 1896, in which he defended his actions. He passed away in 1902 at the age of eighty-two in Gainesville and is buried in Alta Vista Cemetery.

General Robert E. Lee skillfully withdrew his army out of Pennsylvania after the battle and back to Virginia, where he took up defensive positions around Richmond. In 1864, Lee would face off against Ulysses S. Grant, who planned a massive campaign of maneuver and attrition against all Confederate armies with the aim to capture Richmond. Lee's army fought heroically but was eventually forced to abandon Richmond and Petersburg, retreating westward toward Appomattox, where they were nearly surrounded in April of 1865 by Grant's forces. Lee agreed to Grant's generous terms of surrender for his army. After the war Lee became the president of what is now Washington and Lee University and was a leading advocate of reconciliation with the North. He died in 1870 at the age of sixty-three in Lexington, Virginia, and is buried at the Lee Chapel at Washington and Lee University. Lee's citizenship was restored after a joint resolution of the U.S. Senate in 1975.

PRESIDENT ABRAHAM LINCOLN

Abraham Lincoln won re-election in 1864 by a landslide, aided greatly by major victories on the battlefield at the end of that year. The last few months of his life were devoted to passing the Thirteenth Amendment to abolish slavery and to bring an end to the war. In March 1865, just weeks before Lee's surrender at Appomattox, Lincoln met with Generals Grant and Sherman and Admiral Porter aboard the River Queen to discuss the end of hostilities. Lincoln made his intentions clear: "I want no one punished." These simple instructions paved the way for an end to the bloodshed and the start of reconciliation between North and South. A few weeks later, on April 14, Lincoln was assassinated at Ford's Theater in Washington, DC, by the actor John Wilkes Booth, a Confederate sympathizer. The Thirteenth Amendment to end slavery was passed by the Senate on April 8, 1864, by the House on January 31, 1865, and adopted on December 6, 1865.

"*With malice toward none; with charity for all; with firmness in the right, as God gives us to see the right, let us strive on to finish the work we are in; to bind up the nation's wounds; to care for him who shall have borne the battle, and for his widow, and his orphan—to do all which may achieve and cherish a just, and a lasting peace, among ourselves, and with all nations.*"

—Abraham Lincoln

Appendix A

ARMY OF THE POTOMAC ORDER OF BATTLE

First Corps, commanded by Maj. Gen. John F. Reynolds, with divisions commanded by Brig. Gen. James S. Wadsworth, Brig. Gen. John C. Robinson, and Maj. Gen. Abner Doubleday.

Second Corps, commanded by Maj. Gen. Winfield S. Hancock, with divisions commanded by Brig. Gens. John C. Caldwell, John Gibbon, and Alexander Hays.

Third Corps, commanded by Maj. Gen. Daniel E. Sickles, with divisions commanded by Maj. Gen. David B. Birney and Maj. Gen. Andrew A. Humphreys.

Fifth Corps, commanded by Maj. Gen. George Sykes (George G. Meade until June 28. 1863), with divisions commanded by Brig. Gens. James Barnes, Romeyn B. Ayres, and Samuel W. Crawford.

Sixth Corps, commanded by Maj. Gen. John Sedgwick, with divisions commanded by Brig. Gen. Horatio G. Wright, Brig. Gen. Albion P. Howe, and Maj. Gen. John Newton.

Eleventh Corps, commanded by Maj. Gen. Oliver O. Howard, with divisions commanded by Brig. Gen. Francis C. Barlow, Brig. Gen. Adolph von Steinwehr, and Maj. Gen. Carl Schurz.

Twelfth Corps, commanded by Maj. Gen. Henry W. Slocum, with divisions commanded by Brig. Gens. Alpheus S. Williams and John W. Geary.

Cavalry Corps, commanded by Maj. Gen. Alfred Pleasonton, with divisions commanded by Brig. Gens. John Buford, David McMurtrie Gregg, and H. Judson Kilpatrick.

Artillery Reserve, commanded by Brig. Gen. Robert O. Tyler. (The preeminent artillery officer at Gettysburg was Brig. Gen. Henry J. Hunt, chief of artillery on Meade's staff.)

Union Casualties at Gettysburg:

Killed: 3,155

Wounded: 14,531

Missing: 5,369

Total: 23,055

(from *Regimental Strengths and Losses at Gettysburg* by John W. Busey and David G. Martin.)

ARMY OF NORTHERN VIRGINIA ORDER OF BATTLE

First Corps, commanded by Lt. Gen. James Longstreet, with divisions commanded by Maj. Gens. Lafayette McLaws, George E. Pickett, and John Bell Hood.

Second Corps, commanded by Lt. Gen. Richard S. Ewell, with divisions commanded by Maj. Gens. Jubal A. Early, Edward "Allegheny" Johnson, and Robert E. Rodes.

Third Corps, commanded by Lt. Gen. A. P. Hill, with divisions commanded by Maj. Gens. Richard H. Anderson, Henry Heth, and W. Dorsey Pender.

Cavalry division, commanded by Maj. Gen. J. E. B. Stuart, with brigades commanded by Brig. Gens. Wade Hampton, Fitzhugh Lee, Beverly H. Robertson, Albert G. Jenkins, William E. "Grumble" Jones, and John D. Imboden, and Col. John R. Chambliss.

Confederate Casualties at Gettysburg:

Killed: 4,708

Wounded: 12,693

Missing: 5,830

Total: 23,231

Appendix B

GETTYSBURG: INTERESTING FACTS AND TRIVIA

ARMY MASCOTS

The dog at the foot of the Irish Brigade's monument at Gettysburg is an Irish wolfhound, the brigade's mascot. Two Irish wolfhounds were adopted by the 69th New York Infantry and were clad in green coats bearing the number "69" in gold letters. They would parade immediately to the rear of the Regimental Color Guard. Most Civil War units, North and South, often adopted a mascot of some kind—dogs, cats, birds, bears, raccoons, badgers, and in one case, a camel.

THE UNION CHEER VS. THE REBEL YELL

The Irish Brigade was famous for its war cry, "Faugh a ballagh," which means "clear the way." Many Union units had their own war cries, and Union soldiers were famous for cheering on the battlefield to celebrate victory, or on occasion, to salute the gallantry of an enemy unit.

The Confederate troops preferred their own form of battle cry called "the rebel yell." It is said to be a high pitched "Wa-woo-woohoo, wa-woo woohoo" almost always reserved for the attack. Shelby Foote notes that historians are not quite sure how the yell sounded, being described as "a foxhunt yip mixed up with sort of a banshee squall." Union Soldiers described the yell with reference to "a peculiar corkscrew sensation that went up your spine when you heard it," along with the comment that "if you claim you heard it and weren't scared that means you never heard it."

THE AMAZING DANIEL SICKLES

Before the Civil War, Union General Dan Sickles shot and killed Phillip Barton Key, the son of Francis Scott Key in Lafayette Park in Washington, DC, over an alleged romance with Sickles's wife. Sickles was acquitted of the murder by using the "not guilty by reason of insanity" defense, the first American to successfully make such a plea. One of his defense lawyers was Edwin M. Stanton, who became Secretary of War under President Lincoln. Sickles's severed leg bone from his wounding at Gettysburg is still on display at the National Museum of Health and Medicine. He outlived all the other general officers who fought at Gettysburg, passing away on May 3, 1914, at the age of ninety-four, in New York City.

THE UNION'S "MEDAL OF HONOR" VS. THE CONFEDERATE "ROLL OF HONOR"

On July 12, 1862, Congress passed a resolution to establish the Medal of Honor for military personnel who "distinguished themselves by their gallantry in action." Sixty-three soldiers received this award for their actions at Gettysburg, including Colonel Joshua Lawrence Chamberlain.

The Confederate Congress authorized a Confederate Medal of Honor in October 1862, but no official awards for gallantry were ever issued to soldiers. Instead a "Roll of Honor" was established to contain the names of deserving soldiers selected one-per-company by their peers at each engagement. To be "mentioned in dispatches" on official after-action reports was a great honor.

ABRAHAM LINCOLN

Lincoln was the tallest president. At 6 feet, 4 inches, Lincoln towered over most other people. The average height for a man during that time was about 5 feet, 6 inches. When seated, the president was about the same height as an average man; he just had exceptionally long legs. His height and appearance were often the subject of jokes he made about himself, which he used with great effect to gain the attention of onlookers before a speech. One of his favorite jokes was, "If I were two-faced, would I be wearing this one?"

Lincoln's stovepipe top hat served as more than fashionable headgear. He used it to store and carry notes, letters, and even bills. It is said he liked to wear his tall hat in order to be easily seen in a crowd and to stand above his political rivals.

Before Abraham Lincoln, there had never been a U.S. president with a beard. Since his presidency, four presidents have had full beards.

Abraham Lincoln and Jefferson Davis, President of the Confederate States of America, were born only a few dozen miles apart from each other in Kentucky.

Abraham Lincoln was the first president to be born outside of the original thirteen states.

Lincoln was a deeply religious Christian, but never formally joined any church. He read the Bible often. When asked if he thought the Lord was on the side of the North in the Civil War, Lincoln responded, "I am not at all concerned about that . . . But it is my constant anxiety and prayer that I and this nation should be on the Lord's side."

In February of 1862, Lincoln turned down an offer by the King of Siam to send a herd of elephants to help the Union win the Civil War. Lincoln kindly replied, "I appreciate most highly Your Majesty's tender of good offices in forwarding to this Government a stock from which a supply of elephants might be raised on our own soil . . . Our political jurisdiction, however, does not reach latitude so low as to favor the multiplication of the elephant . . ."

Acknowledgments

Special thanks to Fritz Heinzen and Julie Matysik, who were ever supportive in writing this book. Also, I wish to give a heartfelt thank you to my wife, Chona, for her vast reserves of patience being married to a Civil War historian.

Special thanks also to Leon Reed, Ken Giorlando, Jen Goellnitz, Dana Juriew, John Heiser and the Gettysburg National Military Park, Becky Ceravolo and the Snite Museum of Art, Don Troiani and Robin Feret at Historical Art Prints, Mike Campbell, and Sara Kitchen.

Glossary

abolish: to do away with; put an end to; annul; make void: to abolish slavery.

abolitionist: a person who advocated or supported the abolition of slavery in the United States.

absolution: a remission of sin or of the punishment for sin, made by a priest.

allegiances: loyalty or devotion to some person, group, cause, or the like.

amnesty: a general pardon for offenses, especially political offenses, against a government.

audacity: boldness or daring, especially with confident or arrogant disregard for personal safety.

bedizened: to dress or adorn in a showy, gaudy, or tasteless manner.

beseech: to beg eagerly for; solicit.

blunder: a gross, stupid, or careless mistake.

bombardment: to attack or batter with artillery fire.

border states: the slave states of Delaware, Maryland, Kentucky, and Missouri, which refused to secede from the Union in 1860–1861.

breastworks: a defensive work of wood and or stone, usually breast high.

brevity: shortness of time or duration.

brigade: a military unit having its own headquarters and consisting of two or more regiments.

caisson: a two-wheeled wagon, used for carrying artillery ammunition.

calamity: grievous affliction; adversity; misery; *the calamity of war.*

canister: a shaped metal charge filled with small metal balls fired at close range against infantry.

cannonade: a continued discharge of cannon, especially during an attack.

cantankerous: disagreeable to deal with; contentious; peevish; argumentative.

commenced: to begin; start.

commendation: the act of commending; recommendation; praise.

commissioned: an authoritative order, charge, or direction.

comprehend: to understand the nature or meaning of; grasp with the mind; perceive.

conflagration: a destructive fire, usually an extensive one.

consecrated: to make (something) an object of honor or veneration; hallow.

converge: to tend to meet in a point or line; incline toward each other.

corps: a military unit of ground combat forces consisting of two or more divisions.

counsels: advice; opinion or instruction given in directing the judgment or conduct of another.

courier: a messenger, usually traveling in haste, bearing urgent news.

cupola: a light structure on a dome or roof, serving as a belfry, lantern, or belvedere.

decisive: having the power or quality of deciding; crucial or most important.

demise: termination of existence or operation: *the demise of the empire.*

demoralized: to deprive (a person or persons) of spirit, courage, discipline, etc.

deployed: to arrange in a position of readiness, or to move strategically or appropriately.

deprive: to remove or withhold something from the enjoyment or possession of.

detachment: the act of sending out a detached force of troops; a separate group.

dictator: a person exercising absolute power.

dire: causing or involving great fear or suffering; dreadful; terrible: *a dire calamity.*

discretionary: subject or left to one's own discretion; their own choice.

distraught: distracted; deeply agitated; upset.

diversionary: to divert or distract the attention; *a diversionary attack.*

elite: representing the most choice or select; best: an elite group of soldiers.

eloquence: the practice or art of using language with fluency and aptness.

emancipation: the act of emancipating; to free someone from slavery.

en echelon: a formation of troops in which groups of soldiers are arranged in parallel lines, either with each line extending to the right of the one in front (right echelon) or with each line extending to the left of the one in front (left echelon) so that the whole presents the appearance of steps.

enfilade: a position of works, troops, etc., making them subject to a sweeping fire from along the length of a line of troops, a trench, a battery, etc.

exultant: exulting; highly elated; jubilant; triumphant.

firebrand: a person who kindles strife or encourages unrest; an agitator; troublemaker.

flank: the extreme right or left side of an army or military unit.

forsakes: to quit or leave entirely; abandon; desert.

gallant: brave, spirited, noble-minded, or chivalrous.

guile: insidious cunning in attaining a goal; crafty or artful deception; duplicity.

havoc: great destruction or devastation; ruinous damage.

humiliating: lowering the pride, self-respect, or dignity of a person; mortifying.

hypocrisy: a pretense of having a virtuous character, moral or religious beliefs or principles, etc., that one does not really possess.

initiative: an introductory act or step; leading action; readiness and ability in initiating action.

keynote: the main idea or central principle of a speech, program, thought, action, etc.

laden: burdened; loaded down.

levied: an imposing or collecting, as of a tax, by authority or force.

militia: a body of citizen volunteer soldiers as distinguished from professional soldiers.

morale: emotional or mental condition with respect to cheerfulness, confidence, zeal, etc.

muster: to assemble troops as for battle, display, inspection, orders, or discharge.

Napoleons: cannons of the Napoleonic era designed to fire twelve-pound projectiles.

Navarre: a reference to Henry of Navarre (Henry IV), King of France in 1610.

oration: a formal public speech, especially one delivered on a special occasion.

outflank: to outmaneuver or bypass.

perpetuate: to preserve from extinction or oblivion: to perpetuate one's name.

pickets: a soldier or detachment of soldiers placed on a line forward of a position to warn against an enemy advance.

portico: a structure consisting of a roof supported by columns or piers; a porch.

practicable: capable of being done, effected, or put into practice, with the available means.

premise: a basis, stated or assumed, on which reasoning proceeds.

proclamation: something that is proclaimed; a public and official announcement.

prominence: something that is prominent; a projection: *a prominence high over a ravine.*

prophecies: the foretelling or prediction of what is to come.

protégé: a person under the patronage, protection, or care of someone interested in his or her career or welfare.

provisions: a supply or stock of something provided; usually refers to food.

railway cut: where a hill has been excavated to allow the passage of a train,

rallied: to bring into order again; gather and organize or inspire anew.

reconcile: to win over to friendliness; to reconcile hostile persons.

reconnaissance: a search made for useful military information in the field, especially by examining the ground.

recriminations: the act of recriminating, or countercharging; assigning blame.

redemption: deliverance; rescue; atonement for guilt.

regiment: a unit of ground forces, consisting of two or more companies.

reinforce: to strengthen (a military force) with additional troops.

sacred: reverently dedicated to some person, purpose, object, or religious purpose.

scolded: to find fault with angrily; chide; reprimand.

siege: the act or process of surrounding and attacking a fortified place in such a way as to isolate it from help and supplies, for the purpose of lessening the resistance of the defenders and thereby making capture possible.

skirmishers: small units of troops, especially advanced or outlying detachments of opposing armies.

squad: a small number of soldiers, commonly ten privates, a staff sergeant, and a corporal.

tactical victory: a victory that results in the completion of an objective as part of a larger operation or campaign.

tantalizing: something that provokes or arouses expectation, interest, or desire, especially that which remains unobtainable or beyond one's reach.

timidity: lacking in self-assurance, courage, or bravery; easily alarmed; timorous; shy.

topographical: the detailed mapping or charting of the features of a relatively small area.

tourniquet: any device for arresting bleeding by forcibly compressing a blood vessel, as a bandage tightened by twisting.

transcendingly: to rise above or go beyond; overpass; exceed.

typhoid fever: an infectious, often fatal, feverish disease affecting the stomach and intestines.

tyranny: arbitrary or unrestrained exercise of power; despotic abuse of authority.

ultimately: maximum; decisive; conclusive: *the ultimate authority.*

unified: to make or become a single unit; unite: *to unify a country.*

unparalleled: unequaled or unmatched; peerless; unprecedented.

veteran: a person who has served in a military force, especially one who has fought in a war.

withering: to abash, as by a scathing glance.

Bibliography

Alexander, E. Porter. *Fighting for the Confederacy: The Personal Recollections of General Edward Porter Alexander.* Chapel Hill: The University of North Carolina Press, 1989.

—. "Letter From General E. P. Alexander, Late Chief Of Artillery, First Corps., A. N. V." *Southern Historical Society Papers, Vol. IV.* Richmond, Virginia, September, 1877: No. 3.

Alleman, Tillie (Pierce). *Gettysburg, or, What a Girl Saw And Heard of the Battle. A True Narrative.* New York: W. Lake Borland, 1889.

Boritt, S. Gabor. *The Gettysburg Gospel: The Lincoln Speech That Nobody Knows.* New York: Simon & Schuster, 2006.

Burns, Ken. *The Civil War,* PBS, 1990.

Chamberlain, Joshua L. *Through Blood and Fire at Gettysburg.* Gettysburg: Stan Clark Military Books, 1996.

Coffin, Charles C. *The Boys of '61; Or, Four Years of Fighting: Personal Observation with the Army and Navy, From the First Battle of Bull Run to the Fall of Richmond.* Boston: Estes and Laurat, 1886.

Foote, Shelby. *The Civil War: A Narrative: Volume 2: Fredericksburg to Meridian.* New York: Vintage, 1986.

—. *Stars in Their Courses: The Gettysburg Campaign, June–July 1863.* New York: Modern Library, 1994.

Frassanito, William A. *Gettysburg: A Journey in Time.* Gettysburg: Thomas Publications, 1996.

Freeman, Douglas S. *Lee.* New York: Scribner, 1997.

Fremantle, Arthur J. L. *Three Months in the Southern States: April, June, 1863.* Mobile: S. H. Goetzel, 1864: Call number 2670 Conf. (Rare Book Collection, University of North Carolina at Chapel Hill).

Gallagher, Gary W. *Two Witnesses at Gettysburg: The Personal Accounts of Whitelaw Reid and A. J. L. Fremantle.* New York: Wiley-Blackwell, 2009.

Haskell, Aretas. *Battle of Gettysburg.* Wisconsin History Commission, 1908.

Imboden, John. "The Confederate Retreat From Gettysburg." *Battles and Leaders of the Civil War, Vol. IV.* Robert Underwood Johnson, Clarence Clough Buel, New York: The Century Co., 1888.

Johnson, Clifton. *Battlefield Adventures: The Stories of Dwellers on the Scenes of Conflict in Some of the Most Notable Battles of the Civil War.* Boston & New York: Houghton Mifflin, The Riverside Press, Cambridge, 1915.

Kidd, James Harvey. *Personal Recollections of a Cavalryman With Custer's Michigan Cavalry Brigade in the Civil War.* Ionia: Sentinel Printing Co., 1908.

Kohl, Lawrence. *Memoirs of Chaplain Life: Three Years with the Irish Brigade in the Army of the Potomac.* New York: Fordham University Press, 1992.

Law, Evander M. "Struggle for the Round Top." *Battles and Leaders of the Civil War, Vol. III.* Robert Underwood Johnson, Clarence Clough Buel, New York: The Century Co., 1888.

Lee, Robert E., Jr. *Recollections and Letters of General Robert E. Lee.* New York: Doubleday, Page & Co., 1904.

Longacre, Edward G. *General John Buford: A Military Biography.* Boston: Da Capo Press, 2003.

Longstreet, James. *From Manassas to Appomattox.* Philadelphia: Lippincott, 1915.

—. "Lee's Invasion of Pennsylvania." *Battles and Leaders of the Civil War, vol. III.* Robert Underwood Johnson, Clarence Clough Buel, New York: The Century Co., 1888.

—. "Lee's Right Wing at Gettysburg." *Battles and Leaders of the Civil War, Vol. III.* Robert Underwood Johnson, Clarence Clough Buel, New York: The Century Co., 1888.

McPherson, James M. *Hallowed Ground: A Walk at Gettysburg.* New York: Crown, 2003.

Meade, George. *The Life and Letters of George Gordon Meade.* New York: Scribner's Sons, 1913.

Mingus, Scott. *Human Interest Stories of the Gettysburg Campaign—Vols I&II.* Orrtanna: Colecraft Industries, 2006–07.

Moat, Adrian. *Gettysburg.* The History Channel, 2001.

Morris, Errol. "Whose Father Was He?" *The New York Times,* March 29, 2009.

Piston, William G. *Lee's Tarnished Lieutenant: James Longstreet and His Place in Southern History.* Athens: University of Georgia Press, 1990.

Sears, Stephen W. *Gettysburg.* New York: Houghton Mifflin, 2003.

Sheldon, George. *When the Smoke Cleared at Gettysburg.* Nashville: Cumberland House, 2003.

Skelly, Daniel. *A Boy's Experiences During the Battle of Gettysburg.* Gettysburg: Self Published, 1932.

Sorrel, Moxley G. *Recollections of a Confederate Staff Officer.* New York: The Neale Publishing Company, 1905.

Stewart, George. *Pickett's Charge, A Microhistory of the Final Attack at Gettysburg, July 3, 1863.* New York: Houghton Mifflin Co., 1991.

Stewart, Salome M. and Sarah S. Rogers. *The Ties of the Past : The Gettysburg Diaries of Salome Myers Stewart, 1854–1922.* Gettysburg: Thomas Publications, 1996.

Thomas, Emory M. *Robert E. Lee: A Biography.* New York: W. W. Norton & Company, 1995.

Trobriand, Régis. *Four Years with the Army of the Potomac.* Boston: Ticknor and Company, 1889.

Wert, Jeffry D. *Cavalryman of the Lost Cause: A Biography of J. E. B. Stuart.* New York: Simon & Schuster, 2008.

RECOMMENDED READING FOR YOUNG ADULTS

The Private History of a Campaign That Failed by Mark Twain

The Red Badge of Courage by Stephen Crane

The Long Road to Gettysburg by Jim Murphy

The Killer Angels by Michael Shaara

Stars in Their Courses: The Gettysburg Campaign, June–July 1863 by Shelby Foote

Hallowed Ground: A Walk at Gettysburg by James M. McPherson

Human Interest Stories of the Gettysburg Campaign—Vols I&II by Scott Mingus

ADDITIONAL TITLES BY IAIN C. MARTIN

The Greatest U.S. Marine Corps Stories Ever Told

The Greatest U.S. Army Stories Ever Told

The Greatest U.S. Navy Stories Ever Told

Worthy of Their Esteem: The Timeless Words and Sage Advice of Abraham Lincoln

With Strong and Active Faith: The Wisdom of Franklin Delano Roosevelt

The Quotable American Civil War

Index